What I Wish
I Knew About
LUCK

What I Wish I Knew About

LUCK

A Crash Course on Turning
Aspirations into Achievements

Tina Seelig

HARPERONE

An Imprint of HarperCollins*Publishers*

The names and identifying characteristics of some individuals in this book have been changed to protect their privacy.

HarperCollins books may be purchased for educational, business, or sales promotional use. For information, please email the Special Markets Department at SPsales@harpercollins.com.

hc.com

FIRST EDITION

Designed by Jason Kayser

Library of Congress Cataloging-in-Publication Data has been applied for.

ISBN 978-0-06-347136-8

Printed in the United States of America

26 27 28 29 30 LBC 5 4 3 2 1

To my father, for his hundredth birthday!
I'm so fortunate to be your daughter.
XOXO

CONTENTS

**PART 3
Hoist Your Sail**

Introduction

Catching the Winds of Luck

In September 1934, my then eight-year-old father looked out from the deck of the SS *New York* with his parents, grandmother, and younger brother. They had fled the growing threats in Nazi Germany in search of safety, freedom, and the promise of a new life in the United States. The voyage had been calm, but as the Statue of Liberty came into view, their hope was suddenly shaken.

When immigration officials boarded the ship to inspect passenger documents and perform health checks, most families were cleared to continue to Manhattan. But my grandfather's name was called. Something was wrong. Their family was ordered off the ship and transported, along with all their belongings, to Ellis Island. Confused and anxious, my grandparents were told their financial sponsorship had been rejected. The documents provided by my father's Aunt Sophie, which had secured their visas months earlier in Germany, were no longer valid.

The reason was a devastating technicality: Aunt Sophie had recently separated from her husband, and he had withdrawn his financial guarantee. Without it, US Immigration considered my family a potential burden. They were now immigrants without a country, so close to America's shores, yet suddenly at risk of being sent back.

Faced with the unthinkable—a return to Germany—Aunt Sophie acted. With time running short, she launched a desperate search for my grandfather's long-lost brother, Uncle Leo. They hadn't seen him in years and had no address or phone number. All they had was a rumor that he might be a butcher somewhere in the Bronx and that he had changed his last name from Seelig to Singer.

Somehow, against all odds, Aunt Sophie found Uncle Leo by calling every single butcher in the Bronx. Learning of my family's circumstances, he rushed to Ellis Island just in time and offered to step in. Uncle Leo swore he would support his brother's family. But the officials remained unmoved . . . until one noticed Uncle Leo's lapel. He was wearing a Freemason pin, representing a fraternal order that evolved from the guilds of stonemasons and cathedral builders in medieval Europe.

"You're a Mason?" the officer asked.

Uncle Leo nodded. "Yes, I hold a minor rank."

The official paused, then smiled. "So do I."

That moment changed everything. On September 14, 1934, my father and his family finally stepped onto American soil. It was indeed the beginning of a new life, one that my father claims has been propelled by luck.

My father and I have debated the role of luck in our lives for decades. He insists that so many of the pivotal moments in his life, including being rescued at Ellis Island, marrying my mother, and building a successful career, were the result of unexpected doors swinging open at just the right time. He credits these events to forces beyond his control. But I see it differently. From my vantage point, watching my father, I believe that he didn't just stumble into luck. He created it by cultivating attitudes and actions that made him ready when opportunities appeared.

My belief stems from years of teaching entrepreneurship at Stanford University, where I have witnessed many hundreds of students learn how to bring their dreams to fruition. They learn how to identify problems and opportunities, generate innovative solutions, test those ideas, cultivate effective teams, build on success, and bounce back from disappointments. They essentially learn how to be lucky.

There is an art and a science to luck. Those who are lucky know how to see and seize the possibilities that are often invisible to others. They understand that luck is abundant, waiting to be uncovered, including life-altering opportunities such as starting a company that grows into a thriving venture, identifying a compound that proves to be a cure for a rare disease, or meeting their life partner by starting a conversation with the person standing next to them while in line for coffee.

Unfortunately, most people leave valuable opportunities untapped by walking away from possibilities that are right in front of them which, if seen and seized, could lead to incredibly lucky breaks. They throw away chances because they don't recognize or utilize the luck-enhancing skills they already possess or could easily learn. Instead, they resign themselves to the belief that they're unlucky. The consequence is extensive untapped potential, abandoned goals, and a growing gap between aspirations and achievements.

Capturing luck is a skill that can be mastered. The key is understanding the physics of luck and how to apply it to reach your goals. There is no magic. We live in a world of cause and effect. What you do determines what happens next. However, like gravity, luck is invisible, and you need to trust that it is there. Mastering the underlying mechanics of how the world works enables you to harness the abundant opportunities that surround you.

Recognizing and acting upon opportunities often require taking a calculated risk. The smallest choices, such as striking up a conversation at a coffee shop, can unlock a chain of events that can lead to extraordinary outcomes. In fact, this book is a testament to that truth. It all began with a conversation with the man seated next to me on a very early morning flight eighteen years ago. Had I chosen to put on my headphones and drift off to sleep, this book, and the three before it, might not exist. That story, which I share in chapter 13, demonstrates how a single conversation can change your life.

Introducing yourself is just one way to invite luck into your world. There are dozens of approaches that can turn the merely possible into the highly probable. Learning to recognize and use these tools will unleash opportunities every single day. At its core, catching luck requires a belief that there is a prize in every room and it is up to you to find it.

So, What Is Luck?

The definition of luck is "success or failure apparently brought on by chance rather than through one's own actions."[1] The keyword here is *apparently*. This is where most people misunderstand luck. They believe it is out of their control. However, the reality is far more empowering: What we call "luck" is the result of deliberate actions and consistent efforts. It may appear to be brought on by chance, since actions and efforts often happen behind the scenes. The resulting misconception creates a misguided mindset that we must passively wait for good luck to arrive at our doorstep, instead of stepping outside to find it.

Let's start by clarifying the definitions of fortune and luck I will use in this book, which are critically important to understanding what you can and can't control. These concepts are distinct, yet they're frequently used interchangeably. The resulting confusion about cause and effect undermines our ability to see and secure lucky opportunities.

Fortune is an external force, outside of your control. For instance, you might be fortunate to be born in a city with a wealth of resources, such as great schools and abundant jobs. Or you might be unfortunate to have the opposite. Fortune—good or bad—happens to you.

Luck, on the other hand, is the result of choices you make and chances that you take. For example, if you are fortunate to live somewhere with abundant jobs, you are lucky when you receive an attractive job offer. The offer is the fruit of your decisions and actions, including gaining the required skills, tailoring your résumé, writing a compelling cover letter, and nailing the interview. Luck happens because you build a path to its door.

Luck requires taking a chance—a calculated risk. It begins the moment you decide to act in the face of uncertainty. Whether it's throwing your hat into the ring for a competitive opportunity, moving to a distant city without a clear plan, or simply introducing yourself to someone new, each action is a leap beyond the familiar. These moments may seem small, but they're pivotal, creating openings to capture lucky opportunities.

It is just as important to distinguish between chance and gambling as it is to distinguish between fortune and luck. When you take a chance, you have some control over the outcome. For example, when you ask someone out on a date or apply for a job, you are taking a chance. There is a risk that the other person will say no or that you won't be offered an interview. However, if you ask politely and write a compelling cover letter, respectively, you increase the probability of getting a positive response. This is critically important: You take a chance when you have a measurable amount of influence over the outcome.

Gambling differs from chance because the outcome is purely random. Buying a lottery ticket, for example, is different from playing poker. Poker is a game of chance, since you can improve your odds of winning by learning how to play the game better. A skilled poker player is much more likely to win than a novice. However, your odds of having a winning lottery ticket are completely random; they do not improve with preparation, skill, or experience.

Another related term is *serendipity*—a fortunate event that can be leveraged to create a lucky outcome.[2] For example, you would be fortunate to bump into an old friend while traveling in a foreign city. You can turn that fortunate event into a lucky one when you take a small risk, such as asking them what they are doing that evening, learning that they are going to a party, and being invited to join them. At that party, you might meet your new best friend. That is serendipity.

The word *serendipity* is derived from a Persian fairy tale, *The Three Princes of Serendip*.[3] In the tale, originally written in 1302, three princes travel abroad and, by observing subtle clues along the road, deduce details about a camel they have never seen. Among a long list of observations, they note that grass is eaten only on one side of the path, suggesting to them that the camel is blind in one eye; lumps of unchewed grass hint of a missing tooth; and the presence of ants on one side of the road and flies on the other makes them believe that the animal is carrying butter on one side and honey on the other. When the missing camel is eventually found, their deductions are proven correct, and they are richly rewarded. The salient lesson from this tale is that while all the information was available—how fortunate—it took curiosity and careful observation to turn clues into useful conclusions—how lucky!

A more modern example of serendipity comes from the development of Post-it Notes at 3M.[4] These now ubiquitous sticky notes are the result of seeing the opportunities in a failed attempt to make a strong adhesive. Instead of throwing away the glue that didn't stick well, the inventor, Spencer Silver, continued to search for ways it could be used. One day, Art Fry, another scientist at 3M, realized that the adhesive could be used for removable bookmarks in his choir's hymnal. Together they developed Post-its. This is a case of serendipity: a combination of fortunate events that were leveraged to create a lucky outcome. The minimally sticky glue was a fortunate discovery developed by accident. Building a market for this unusual glue, created by Fry and Silver, was lucky.

Understanding the distinctions between luck, fortune, chance, gambling, and serendipity reveals that luck isn't random. What looks arbitrary from the outside is usually the result of deliberate decisions and behaviors. From a distance, some achievements may appear effortless, but they are anything but! As the saying goes, it takes years of hard work for someone to become an "overnight success." According to legend, when the artist Pablo Picasso was asked why he was charging a million francs for a quick sketch that took only minutes to create, he replied, "My dear, it took me a lifetime to be able to draw this sketch."[5]

Don't let the way the word *luck* is used in casual conversation distract you from its real meaning. It is often used as a convenient cover or excuse. Some people downplay their achievements by claiming they're lucky, either out of humility or a lack of awareness of the effort they've invested. Others excuse their disappointments by attributing them to bad luck, deflecting attention from poor judgment or performance.

Two frequently cited adages about luck are true but incomplete:

> "Fortune favors the prepared mind," credited to the scientist Louis Pasteur.

"The harder I work, the luckier I get," attributed to many, including the US president Thomas Jefferson.

These expressions, which will be unpacked throughout this book, are only instructive when you know how to develop a "prepared mind" and what "hard work" entails.

Life Isn't Fair

Of course, not everything is within our control, and life isn't fair. Some people face incredibly tough situations that can feel impossible to overcome. Earthquakes, floods, fires, wars, and pandemics turn your world upside down. Additional challenges come in many forms, including genetic predispositions, serious health problems, complicated family dynamics, financial struggles, and physically and/or emotionally toxic environments. The playing field isn't level, and some must fight much harder just to get by. For some individuals, even the most basic goals, such as feeling safe, staying healthy, or finding stability, feel out of reach. Plus, systemic cultural biases can work against you. The deck is stacked.

For eight years I volunteered at San Quentin State Prison[6] in Northern California, helping the men in The Last Mile program prepare for a life after incarceration by teaching them skills related to entrepreneurship. Hearing their individual stories was heartbreaking. Most of these men started life in terrible circumstances, with poverty, addiction, and abuse. They lacked hope and direction, and they made destructive choices, including joining gangs and committing crimes, to find support in a troubled community. It was only later in life, during their incarceration, that they learned how to identify and make positive choices instead.

In contrast, some people seem to win the birth lottery. They are blessed with beauty, brains, education, money, and/or connections. They have a head start in life, and they're often unaware that their advantages stem from privileges they didn't earn themselves. As the football coach Barry Switzer quipped, "Some people are born on third base and go through life thinking they hit a triple." This baseball analogy captures how easy it is to mistake fortune for merit. Privilege can make people oblivious to the struggles of others and obscure the role that good fortune has played in their own success. Privilege—a.k.a. good fortune—can create blind spots that diminish empathy,[7] sensitivity to the challenges faced by those who were not born into equally fortunate circumstances, and understanding of how their privilege has influenced their trajectory.

No matter how the world treats you, however, you get to choose how to respond. Your choices, in turn, shape how the world will respond to you. We are each locked in a continuous dance with the world in which we trade off who is leading and who is following. Capturing luck is about learning how to lead in your dance with life. In *Man's Search for Meaning*, Viktor E. Frankl, the famous psychotherapist and Holocaust survivor, described a philosophy that helped him endure his horrific circumstances: He wrote, "Between stimulus and response there is a space. In that space is our power to choose our response. In our response lies our growth and our freedom."[8]

Even in the direst situations, there are often opportunities. It is up to you to find them. Those possibilities don't have red flashing neon signs identifying them, and nobody will tell you when you walk right past them. Instead, over time, if you don't harness the luck in your environment, you won't reach your goals, and other individuals will seem to have all the luck. This is not inevitable. You can learn to be lucky.

The Winds of Luck

Luck is like the wind, often unpredictable, and always in motion. You can't control when or where it gusts, but you can learn to identify it and harness its power. Like the captain of a sailing ship, your task is to prepare for luck and to position yourself to catch it when it arrives. There are three essential steps to catching the winds of luck:

- **Construct your ship.** This is your *prepared mind*. It includes your core values, your skills, your risk profile, the story you tell about yourself, and your short-term and long-term goals.
- **Recruit your crew.** It is important to recognize that *luck rarely sails solo*. Your friends, mentors, and

collaborators are the crew that help you identify and capture opportunities. It is nearly impossible to reach your goals in isolation, without others' support.

- **Hoist your sail.** This is the *hard work* of sailing. It includes specific actions, such as showing up, taking risks, stretching beyond your comfort zone, and recovering from inevitable failures.

Sometimes the winds of luck are a soft, gentle breeze nudging you toward your target. At other times, they come in sudden gusts, forcefully propelling you forward with unexpected momentum. There may be tailwinds that accelerate your journey, making the path ahead seem easier and the effort lighter. Headwinds, on the other hand, can reverse your progress, slow you down, or push you in unintended directions. Rather than fearing headwinds, you can learn to respond to them, setting a new course that might be better than you imagined. There are countless examples of disappointments, such as losing a job or an important relationship, that ultimately opened the door to something much better.

Below are five different ways that individuals engage with the winds of luck, from a purely passive stance to actively seeking out opportunities.

- **Stay Inside:** Some sit on the sidelines and watch the winds of luck out their window. They may even close the shutters, blocking out the view all together.

- **Wind Vane:** Some engage opportunities as though swiveling on an axis, observing lucky opportunities but never making a move.
- **Hot Air Balloon:** Some allow themselves to be carried wherever the winds of luck take them, drifting passively, without personal agency.
- **Windmill:** Some actively engage with the winds of luck, turning gusts into energy. They harness luck in their local environment.
- **Sailboat:** Some chase luck with purpose, skillfully navigating on open seas in search of lucky opportunities that are over the horizon.

These scenarios play out every day around the world. If you were to take a group of young people raised in the same country, town, or even the same family, they will ultimately find themselves in vastly different places later in life. What happened? Naturally differences in genetics and upbringing play a role, as do other fortunate and unfortunate events they encounter. However, much of the divergence is attributable to mindset and behavior, including their willingness to take risks, adapt to challenges, and seize opportunities as they arise. In essence, it's their ability to harness the winds of luck that drives outcomes. Where they end up isn't determined solely by their starting points and their good or bad fortune but by how they choose to navigate life's currents.

There are times when the winds of luck are very still,

requiring considerable patience to catch even the faintest breeze. Like a ship stranded in the doldrums, you may find yourself waiting, scanning the horizon, wondering if the wind will ever return. At those times, frustration can creep in and make you doubt if you will ever move forward. But trust that the winds of luck are always shifting. Like a skilled sailor, you can use these lull times to prepare for what's next. Build your ship, recruit your crew, carefully study the currents, and stay ready. Position yourself for moments when the wind picks up again . . . because it will. When it does, you'll be ready to catch it, setting sail toward new horizons, whereas others who aren't prepared will remain stranded. To quote the English historian Edward Gibbon, "The winds and the waves are always on the side of the ablest navigators."

The men in The Last Mile program, for example, were stranded in the doldrums in prison, many for decades. The world outside was passing them by as they waited for a chance to prove their eligibility for parole. While waiting, they prepared for the winds of luck by being model members of the community. Then, when The Last Mile was launched, they were ready. This opportunity, which is only available to those without any disciplinary charges, changes their lives by preparing them for well-paying jobs after they are released. The program gives them the resources to escape a return to prison. These men carefully built their ships, recruited their crew, and hoisted their sails so they would have the best possible opportunity to catch the winds of luck at their parole hearings and upon release.

It is important to remember that building your ship—a *prepared mind*—is not enough to catch luck. You need to sail! Intention setting and positive thinking is necessary but not sufficient to bring good luck your way. While "fortune *favors* the prepared mind," harnessing good luck requires active changes in your behavior. Luck doesn't land in your lap because you're hopeful or smart. It shows up when you act. Your well-built ship can't catch the winds of luck while sitting in the harbor. You need to engage others and leave the safety of the shore.

Fortune and Luck Through the Ages

The concepts of fortune and luck have aroused curiosity and debate throughout recorded history. The ancient Greeks and Romans believed that good fortune was doled out by the gods and goddesses. Fortuna, a Roman goddess, was responsible for the fate and fortune of individuals and cities, and there were temples dedicated to Fortuna throughout the Roman Empire. Statues of Fortuna usually show her holding a cornucopia filled to the brim, signifying abundance, as well as a ship's rudder, indicating her power to steer individual fortunes. This is the origin of the concept of good and bad fortune.[9]

Throughout history, many believed that fortune—good or bad—was part of a divine plan. They believed that good fortune should be received with gratitude and humility, and bad fortune with trust. Many faith traditions also encourage a balance between trust in God and active engagement with the world. As Saint Augustine of Hippo said, "Pray as though everything depended on God. Work as though everything depended on you," and, echoing the framework in this book, he wrote, "God provides the wind, but man must raise the sail." This mindset leads to both respect for the role of God and the need to put in effort.

This idea is vividly illustrated in the Old Testament story of Job in which Satan and God wage a bet involving Job, a wealthy and righteous man. Satan argues that Job's faithfulness depends on his prosperity. In response, God allows Job's faith to be tested. In rapid succession, Job loses everything, including his children, his wealth, his health, and the support of his wife and friends. Despite his suffering and confusion, Job refuses to curse God. He questions what is happening to him and laments the consequences, but he never abandons his faith. In the end, God responds with a reminder of the vastness of divine wisdom. Job's fortunes are ultimately restored, and he lives a long life with renewed prosperity. This story endures as a symbol that misfortune may be part of a purposeful, though mysterious, design.

During the Middle Ages, many symbols and talismans were believed to attract good luck and to fend off bad luck. Horseshoes and four-leaf clovers were widely embraced as good luck charms. These traditions live on today. Another practice that has endured is the custom of saying "God bless you" after someone sneezes. At the time, sneezing was believed to leave a person vulnerable to Satan's influence, and the blessing served as spiritual protection from illness. Bad luck was abundant and could result from breaking a mirror, having a black cat cross your path, or receiving the "evil eye"—a malevolent glare—from someone who wishes you harm.

Many superstitions about luck and fortune exist today. For example, some cultures believe that eating certain foods on New Year's Day will bring good fortune for the coming year. This includes the Chinese tradition of eating long noodles to ensure a long life; eating pomegranate seeds for fertility and vitality; eating lentils—which look like coins—for prosperity; eating ring-shaped food—like donuts—to bring a full year of good fortune; and the Spanish tradition of eating "12 grapes in the 12 seconds after the clock strikes midnight on New Year's Eve [to] ensure 12 months of good things in the coming year."[10]

Even NASA employs lucky charms. After six failed rocket launches to the moon in the early 1960s, the first successful mission was launched on July 28, 1964. What was the difference between the 1964 mission and the ones that preceded it? On the morning of the successful launch, one of the mission engineers passed out peanuts to everyone in the control room to calm nerves. Since then, peanuts have been a staple in the control room for almost all NASA missions, fueling the belief that peanuts are a powerful precursor to good luck.[11]

Philosophers throughout history have pondered the role of luck in our lives. Much of the debate concerns how bad and good luck affect an individual's responsibility for their actions. The famed primatologist Robert Sapolsky investigates this subject in his book *Determined*. Based on Sapolsky's studies of animal and human behavior, he concludes that there is no such thing as free will. Instead, he believes that we are all driven to act by factors outside of our direct control, beginning with our genetics and in utero experiences. In his view, you can't make your own luck. You are born either fortunate or not. He writes, "We are nothing more or less than the cumulative biological and environmental luck, over which we had no control, that has brought us to any moment."[12]

I reached out to Sapolsky to question whether he thought we have any control over luck in our lives. At the end of our lengthy discussion, I conceded that our biology and circumstances bound the possibilities for each of us to some extent. However, as a neuroscientist who spent many years trying to unravel how the brain works, I posit that just because we don't understand consciousness yet does not mean that we lack the ability to change our lives. While you can't do everything, you can do something! Each of us makes choices every day, and we often make dramatic shifts in our behavior based on fresh insights from our experiences. In fact, the goal of this book is to demonstrate that you can change your mind and behavior to get you closer to your short-term and long-term objectives.

Beyond philosophy, behavioral science research on luck demonstrates that some individuals are better at harnessing luck than others. Experimental researchers Peter R. Darke and Jonathan L. Freedman found that people who think of themselves as lucky tend to spot more opportunities to harness good luck.[13] This is consistent with the findings of Richard Wiseman, a psychologist who spent a decade studying why some people seem luckier than others. He identified four key factors among consistently lucky people: (1) They're much better at spotting and leveraging chance opportunities when they arise; (2) they trust their gut feelings and act on them; (3) they maintain an optimistic attitude, believing that good things will come their way; and (4) they have the ability to find silver linings in misfortune and turn seeming bad luck into unexpectedly good outcomes. Together, these findings show that luck isn't just about random chance. It's a set of practices that anyone can develop.[14]

Life Is a Luck Laboratory

We all live in a "luck laboratory," where each day offers a chance to experiment by adjusting our sails just a little bit to capture more luck. Lucky prospects often beget future lucky prospects, like the butterfly effect, where one small action causes a cascade of reactions with far-reaching implications. For example, making one new friend opens your world to all their friends and, in turn, their friends; taking a new job opens up a wealth of possibilities within that organization. As I frequently tell my students, "You don't get a job; you get the keys to the building." Once you take on a new role, a brand-new set of opportunities will present themselves. Therefore, the actions you take today shape the landscape of opportunities you'll encounter in the future.

Essentially, when harnessed, good luck bears an ever-expanding array of fruit. It leads to meaningful relationships and advances in your career, and opens the door to unexpected adventures. Being skilled at catching luck doesn't mean you'll avoid every failure or disappointment. It does mean that over time, the odds that you will achieve your goals improve dramatically. By reading and responding to the winds of luck, you will find that lucky breaks are more abundant. At its core, catching the winds of luck leads to a life rich with potential and purpose.

The following chapters detail strategies and tools for identifying and harnessing lucky breaks to create the life you dream to live. It builds on my three prior books, which provide a foundation of attitudes and actions for developing more agency in your life:

- *What I Wish I Knew When I Was 20* is about building an entrepreneurial mindset, giving yourself permission to question established paths while turning obstacles along the way into opportunities.

- *InGenius* presents the Innovation Engine, a framework for ramping up creative problem-solving in individuals, teams, and organizations.
- *Creativity Rules* describes the Invention Cycle, which accelerates the process for moving from the seeds of an idea to implementation.

Part 1 of this book is dedicated to constructing your ship by clarifying your values, understanding the story you tell about yourself, identifying your unique skills, exploring your risk profile, and setting meaningful goals. In essence, I will address what exactly is Pasteur's "prepared mind." Part 2 is dedicated to recruiting your crew by developing meaningful connections with others. This involves asking for what you want, helping others, showing appreciation, demonstrating curiosity, and resolving conflicts. It unpacks how luck is very often carried by the company you keep. Part 3 shifts to hoisting your sail and heading out to sea. That is, the specific actions needed to actually harness luck. These include activities such as taking calculated risks, challenging assumptions, and mastering resilience. This section addresses the *hard work* of sailing your ship, as in "the harder I work, the luckier I get."

Each chapter begins with a short statement that summarizes how the title concept of that chapter contributes to harnessing luck. For example:

Luck favors those who are both prepared and moved to harness opportunities in their midst.

I encourage you to read each chapter with the opening message in mind, since some attitudes and actions described in each chapter are not immediately obvious precursors to luck. Hopefully by the end of each chapter you will understand how each of these approaches contributes to your ability to harness opportunities that you might not have seen and seized before. In addition, each chapter ends with a few questions that are designed to help you assess how you can increase your luck by applying the ideas in that chapter.

Throughout the book I'll share stories about how many of my colleagues and students catch luck in their lives, illustrating these principles. I'm lucky to work with people from around the world who are carving a path toward their goals. Many are part of Knight-Hennessy Scholars (KHS) at Stanford University, a cadre of emerging leaders, many of whom have overcome formidable personal and societal challenges and offer real-life examples of how luck can be cultivated.[15] These scholars aren't just smart; they are extraordinarily resourceful at squeezing opportunities out of even the most difficult situations. I also include a number of my personal experiences with catching luck. I am acutely aware of how fortunate and lucky I am and know that it often appears that I conjure luck out of thin air.

To deepen these insights, I present behavioral science research that sheds light on how and why these practices work, and classroom activities that bring these concepts to life. You will discover how to spot hidden opportunities, take calculated risks, and transform setbacks into stepping stones. You'll also find that concepts discussed in different chapters are frequently interconnected because success often requires combining strategies, such as embracing risk while learning from failure, or asking for what you want while helping others reach their goals.

I'm writing this book because I see so many people unwittingly leave luck on the table, walking past opportunities that are right in front of them. My goal is to demonstrate that luck is ubiquitous and abundant, and that you have far more power to harness it than you might think. I invite you to experiment with the strategies in the chapters ahead and share your experiences with me at WIWIKLuck@gmail.com. Please feel free to let me know which attitudes and actions provided the biggest benefits and which were most surprising.

Remember, luck requires taking calculated risks, getting out of your comfort zone, and actively engaging in your dance with the world.

Enjoy the journey, and good luck!

Part 1

Construct Your Ship

———

Fortune favors the prepared mind.

—Louis Pasteur

1

Build Your Ballast

*Luck favors those whose values keep them
steady in turbulent waters.*

The elevator jerked to an abrupt halt after the woman standing next to me reached over and hit the Emergency Stop button. Confused, I shifted to find out what was happening. She and the man standing next to her turned toward me with an accusatory look and barked, "Are you a spy?"

I had recently started my first job after graduation at a small medical technology company, and my boss had asked me to attend a conference that was being hosted by a competing start-up. Nonchalantly he asked me to represent myself as a PhD student at Stanford, not as an employee of the company. Given that he was my superior, and that I was both inexperienced and naive, I didn't question his request.

I packed my bag and hopped on a flight to Chicago to attend the conference. After picking up a conference badge with my name and stated affiliation, I entered the small presentation hall. At the end of each talk I asked probing questions that I realized later only someone quite familiar with the technology would be able to ask.

Given their suspicions, the conference hosts had called my company to inquire if I worked there. And, of course, the receptionist quickly volunteered that I was away at a conference in Chicago. *Boom*—I was caught! Interrogated in the elevator, stopped between floors, I quickly confessed. I was brusquely escorted out of the building, shaken from the experience. How unlucky!

I immediately realized that I had made a huge mistake. But how did this happen?! It happened because I had not taken even a minute to think about my core values and to consider how to respond when they were tested. I had acted impulsively, wanting to please my new boss. I jumped in feet-first without considering the consequences of my actions. Had I taken even the smallest amount of time to think about it, I would never have misrepresented myself.

Rash decisions like this one are reactive and impulsive. You can live your life reacting, as though you are controlled only by your decision-making reflexes, or you can thoughtfully reflect before acting. In his seminal book *Thinking, Fast and Slow*,[1] Daniel Kahneman states that we have two ways of thinking. One is impulsive and automatic (also known as System 1 thinking), and the other is reflective and deliberate (System 2 thinking). Kahneman shows that we often fall back on System 1 thinking when instead we should take the time to reflect critically. By slowing down and deciding who you want to be in the world, you will not only do the right thing but also start to create the framework for making future decisions.

Clear core values are like ballast at the bottom of your ship, keeping you steady. They ensure that external circumstances don't pull you off track. They also help you discern whether an opportunity, such as going to a conference under false pretenses, aligns with your values or is a tempting distraction taking you off course. Essentially, your values prevent you from sailing in the wrong direction or even capsizing when challenges wash over you. As Roy E. Disney, the cofounder of the Walt Disney Company, said, "When your values are clear to you, making decisions becomes easier."

Jonathan Haidt, a social psychologist at New York University, has explored the powerful relationship between values and the quality of life. In *The Happiness Hypothesis*, he draws from ancient wisdom traditions and modern psychological research to argue that living in alignment with your deeply held principles is one of the surest paths to a meaningful life.[2] When your values serve as an internal compass, they not only boost your overall well-being but also provide resilience during adversity, clarity in decision-making, and authenticity in your actions. This alignment reduces the mental friction that arises when you're pulled in conflicting directions. In this way, values don't just guide you toward happiness; they enhance your ability to notice and seize the right opportunities.

We live in a world where we are often victims of unwanted control by others, tempting us off course. As Robert B. Cialdini describes in his classic *Influence: The Psychology of Persuasion*,[3] we are easily swayed by psychological triggers that incite us to behave in ways that may conflict with our values. Social proof encourages us to emulate the crowd, while authority figures get us to act by projecting confidence and expertise, and scarcity makes us want things we don't really need. To those without clear core values, these triggers can be exploited, while those with well-defined core values are much less vulnerable to this type of manipulation.

Just as I was manipulated by my boss's authority, my husband, Michael, soon after we were married, experienced a boss who tried to get him to act unethically. Claiming that everyone fabricates information and exaggerates claims when responding to requests for proposals from the United States government, Michael was asked to lie about the specifications of products sold by his company. Michael pushed back, but his boss was insistent and wouldn't relent. Michael quit on the spot. This was a lesson for me as well.

When you clearly define your values and put them front of mind, it's much easier to live in alignment with them, to strengthen your sense of self, and to build trust with those around you. Other people are naturally drawn to those with integrity: The more consistently you act with authenticity, the more meaningful the relationships you cultivate will become.

As described in detail in part 2 of this book, luck usually arrives through other people. A recommendation, a collaboration, a door opening at just the right time. These moments aren't random. They emerge from relationships built on genuine respect and shared principles. Like-minded people gravitate toward one another. When you align your actions with your values, you're more likely to attract those who can open pathways that would otherwise remain hidden.

Alignment of your values and actions becomes especially important when you take on a leadership role. James M. Kouzes and Barry Z. Posner, the authors of *Five Practices of Exemplary Leadership*,[4] posit that articulating your core values to your team, and consistently acting in alignment with them, builds trust and credibility. Trust enhances collaboration, reduces conflict, and creates an environment where people feel motivated and empowered to contribute their best. Ultimately trust enables teams to achieve far more together than they could individually.

This concept is explored in a case study I've used with my students for years. Created by Harvard Business School, the case follows the true story of "Daniel Kim," who, serving as the CFO of a start-up technology company, was asked to approve successively larger misappropriations of funds. The CEO was using company money to pay for personal expenses, such as designer shoes for his girlfriend and expensive hotel rooms that were way outside the company's budget. Using every aspect of influence that he could, the CEO tried to convince Kim that the expenses were reasonable and justified. Sadly, Kim was swayed, initially approving small misappropriations, and over time, much larger amounts. The case shows that once you cross the line and compromise your values, you are likely to put up less resistance to doing so in the future.[5] I use this case to teach students how to inoculate themselves against these types of errors with four actionable steps:

- Be very clear about your core values.
- Don't take the bait—small compromises today can lead to bigger ones in the future.
- Create a personal board of advisors to help you evaluate questionable requests.
- Always have an escape path if you are being pushed onto a slippery slope.

I wish I had known this when I started my first job!

Somik Raha conducted research on values-based decision-making while studying at Stanford University School of Engineering. After graduating, he focused on aligning actions with values within organizations. His book *Invaluable* shows how clarity around values enables organizations to make decisions rooted in those values. Doing so builds internal trust and a stronger culture; hones their external reputation; and opens doors to new partnerships, investments, and collaborations.[6]

In his book, Somik shares how he worked with Scholle, a global plastic packaging company. When their collaboration started, the company leadership team was trying to quickly grow in an industry that is often associated with having a negative impact on the environment. The team found themselves uninspired by the possibilities in front of them. Therefore, instead of focusing directly on strategy, Somik led the leadership team through a process of interrogating the core values of the firm.

The team reflected on what made them proud of their work, and they landed on four values: safe, natural, economic, and sustainable. These values became their guiding light as they shared them with the entire company. This, in turn, unlocked ideas that shaped a new strategy with a focus on safe, natural, economic, and sustainable products. The result was remarkable. The company culture seemed to transform overnight. One division grew their annual innovation portfolio from $2 million to $30 million in worth by focusing on the new mission informed by their values. Their closely held values propelled growth and resulted in a stronger brand, stronger partnerships, and increased investments. Defining their values wasn't an intellectual exercise.

The process literally changed the way employees felt about the company. They became a magnet that drew in the right people, the best partners, the most innovative ideas, and attracted luck their way.

Whether it is explicit or implicit, every person and organization has a reputation or brand that reflects their values. Companies spend fortunes building brands so that the world knows what to expect from them. Done well, a brand is infused into every aspect of the product and user experience to clearly, consistently, and positively convey the organization's values. A brand is essentially a promise. As an individual, you too have a brand or reputation that is anchored in your core values, and it lets everyone know what to expect when they engage with you. You can let your reputation materialize on its own or develop it explicitly.

Your reputation is not built overnight. Rather it is cultivated and nourished through consistent actions that reflect your values. Over time, people make decisions on how to deal with you based on your track record. Your consistency allows your reputation to solidify, earning the confidence of those who engage with you. As the investor and philanthropist Warren Buffett wisely pointed out, "It takes twenty years to build a reputation and five minutes to ruin it." This highlights the delicate nature of your reputation. It is an asset that accrues slowly but can be lost in an instant. A misstep, lapse, or deviation from your core values can shatter years of trust, leaving you scrambling to rebuild credibility.

Many are familiar with Elizabeth Holmes, the founder of the health-tech start-up Theranos. Once the darling of Silicon Valley, she was hailed as a young genius. Luminaries flocked to support her and her company, which promised to revolutionize blood testing. However, after faking a product demonstration, she began a slippery descent, misleading investors, regulators, and patients. When the truth came to light, Holmes's story shifted from one of innovation to a cautionary tale of what happens when ambition eclipses ethics.[7]

Reflecting on your core values, and then actively aligning your behavior with them, does more than build and strengthen your integrity. It communicates confidence and authenticity that naturally attracts opportunities your way. Therefore, establishing and defending your core values enables you to distinguish between choices that are lucky—with a higher probability of a positive outcome—and those that aren't. When you act with clarity and purpose, you send a signal to the world, and the world, in turn, responds.

- *What are your core values?*
- *How do they drive your decisions and choices?*
- *How do those choices unlock luck in your life?*

2

Tell Your Tale

Luck favors those whose personal narrative carries them toward favorable seas.

Please form a line, from left to right, indicating how optimistic or pessimistic you are about the future. Far left is most pessimistic, and right is most optimistic.

This is the beginning of an exercise run by my friend and futurist Lisa Kay Solomon, in our Stanford d.school[1] course Inventing the Future. After the students line up, she asks them to take a step forward if they feel that they have control over the future, and to step back if they feel that they have little control. This human-sized 2 x 2 matrix has the following quadrants:

- Upper right—optimistic with a high sense of control
- Lower left—pessimistic with a low sense of control
- Upper left—pessimistic with a high sense of control
- Lower right—optimistic with a low sense of control

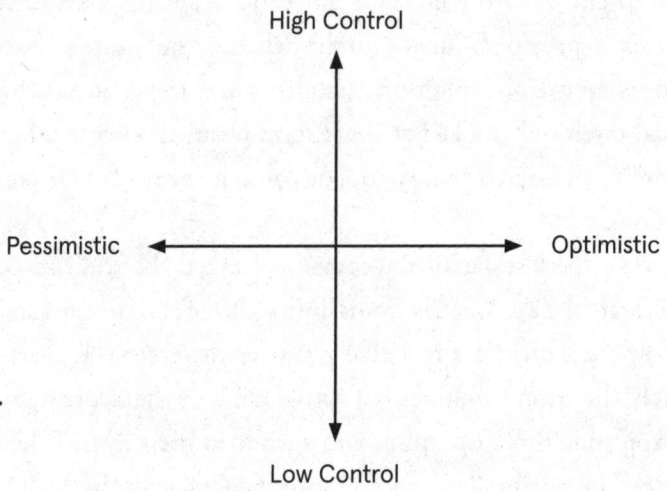

I encourage you to think about where you would place yourself on this matrix. For example, if you are optimistic about the future, you'll fall to the right of the vertical line. If you believe you have control over your future, you'll also be above the horizontal line.

Over the ten-week course, which Lisa and I taught for five years with our colleague Drew Endy, a far-forward-thinking bioengineer, we gave the students lots of opportunities to interrogate the future. For the first five weeks, we taught the students tools for imagining the future and evaluating the potential outcomes. For the second five weeks, students engaged in debates about the utopian and dystopian consequences of a wide range of emerging technologies, including lab-grown meat, mining asteroids, and engineering the weather. We also had a relevant expert join the class each week to provide feedback on the debates. The future scenarios were eye-opening to the students and the experts, who had often only looked at short-term positive outcomes but rarely considered the dystopian consequences of their creations.

On the last day of the course, we asked the students to recreate the 2 x 2 matrix from the first day of class to see if and how their attitudes had changed over the course. Remarkably, the entire group moved considerably to the upper right, expressing more optimism and agency in their lives. When asked for their reflections on those changes, many of the students noted that they used to think that the "future happened to them," and now they understand that they are responsible for shaping the future they want to exist. Nothing about the world had changed, but their attitude toward it had.

This is not surprising. The narrative you create about yourself and the world is constantly evolving. Brian Lowery, a professor at Stanford Graduate School of Business, has done extensive research on how your sense of yourself is influenced by your environment. He notes in his book *Selfless: The Social Creation of "You"*[2] that "the way people behave is as much about where they are as who they are." His research shows that identity is not fixed but rather an ever-changing story influenced by the people around us and the situations we encounter. How others treat us and their expectations shape our sense of self.[3]

This dynamic is vividly illustrated in the "status game." In this exercise, each player is given a standard playing card to hold against their forehead, visible to everyone except themselves. Players are instructed to interact based on each other's perceived "status," with aces, kings, and queens representing high status, and low-numbered cards (such as twos and threes) representing low status. Very quickly the players figure out their own status. High-status individuals attract attention and praise with others eagerly listening to what they have to say. Meanwhile, those assigned low status are usually ignored and/or interrupted. The emotional impact is immediate and palpable, with those with high status feeling empowered and those with low status feeling demoralized. This simple game immediately demonstrates that the stories others tell us about our worth profoundly influence how they treat us and how we feel about ourselves.

Your story, shaped in large part by how others treat you, influences everything you do. It determines whether you see yourself as a passive puppet pulled by external forces or as a powerful puppeteer shaping the world to your will. The truth is, you have the agency to write and rewrite your story. By consciously crafting the narrative about who you are and the control you have over your future, you can transform how you perceive the world, how you engage with it, and how others treat you. Like the students in our class, this shift in perception positions you to actively create a life aligned with your goals and aspirations. Adjusting your story is not merely an act of imagination; it's a bold step toward charting your path to the future.

Dan McAdams, a leading scholar on the power of narrative in our lives, studies how the evolving stories we craft integrate our perceptions, experiences, and aspirations. These narratives help us make sense of our place within the complex social environments in which we live.[4] McAdams emphasizes that we can revise these stories if they no longer serve us. This is an extraordinarily freeing idea! You can re-craft your story from one that is holding you back to one that propels you forward.

Case in point: Andrew Couch, a current Knight-Hennessy scholar, had always shown a natural talent for math. As a homeschooled student, he spent most of his time immersed in equations, believing that language arts and history simply weren't his strengths. He shared this experience during our storytelling program for all first-year scholars. In this program, every new student tells a five-minute story during winter or spring quarters, using communication techniques that they are taught in the fall by our masterful storytelling instructors, Dan Klein and Lisa Rowland.

Andrew told us that when he took the standardized achievement test in fifth grade, the results came as no surprise. He aced the math section but performed poorly in everything else. His mother, disheartened by the lopsided scores, told him he needed to improve. Andrew's first instinct was to shrug it off. "I'm just not good at those subjects." His mother responded with encouragement, stating, "No one starts out being good at anything. It takes practice and a belief that any obstacle can be overcome." Deep down, Andrew realized he was avoiding challenges instead of embracing them. Worse yet, his self-imposed narrative led him to believe that he was inherently weak in language arts. After reflecting on the consequences of this perspective, Andrew began to recognize this self-fulfilling prophecy about his abilities and how it inhibited his otherwise ambitious nature. Andrew decided to change his story and gave himself a personal challenge to dedicate the next year to the subjects he found most difficult.

With this newfound mission to prove his internal narratives wrong, Andrew began to embrace every challenge, choosing to ignore any self-doubt that might undermine his progress. Equipped with study plans and specific goals, and a drive for achieving every goal, Andrew embarked on his journey of self-discovery, finding that he often exceeded his own expectations. One year later, at the end of sixth grade, he took the test again. This time he excelled across the board. Andrew had liberated himself by understanding that the greatest limits we face are often the narratives we tell about what we can and can't accomplish. In his story to the KHS community, his closing line was, "The strongest barriers we face are often the ones we place on ourselves."

It is remarkable how early in our lives we create a story about who we are and what we can accomplish. These stories are shaped by what we see in the world, what we hear from others, and what we feel inside. Over time, these narratives solidify, becoming invisible scripts that guide our decisions, define our boundaries, and shape our sense of possibility. Sometimes they empower us, giving us confidence and clarity. Other times they quietly limit us, keeping us from venturing beyond what we believe is possible. For Andrew, his initial story was limiting, and he needed to put in concerted effort to change it.

Timothy D. Wilson, the author of *Redirect: The Surprising New Science of Psychological Change*,[5] reinforces the importance of actively crafting your personal narrative. He demonstrates that looking at tough times with a different lens can change your story from one that holds you back into one that pushes you forward. Carol S. Dweck's research on mindset[6] also shows that our beliefs about our capabilities profoundly influence our achievements. People who view their abilities as fixed give up when facing challenges, while those with a growth mindset, who believe their capabilities can expand through effort, show remarkable persistence. She proved that simple metaphors, such as describing the brain as a muscle that strengthens with exercise, can fundamentally alter how people view their potential and increase their dedication to achieving their goals.

Examining and editing your personal narrative will empower you to identify which elements serve you well and which are fetters to success. This introspection offers the freedom to discard baggage in your ship, lightening your load and making room for more positively motivating stories. I clearly remember the day I made the deliberate decision to empty my metaphorical suitcase of baggage that I was dragging around, letting go of the stories my parents had told me about how I should be navigating the world. The resulting lightness was palpable and freed me to travel much faster and farther on the path of my choice.

The story you tell yourself about your place in the world shapes everything, including your choices, confidence, and future. Remember, until your last day on earth, your story is always unfolding. I love the quote, attributed to the Irish playwright Oscar Wilde, "It's all good in the end. If it's not good, it's not the end." It is a daily reminder that whatever is happening now, you have the power to write the next chapter.

- *What's your personal narrative about your place in the world?*
- *How does your story enable you to reach your goals, or how does it hold you back?*
- *How might you modify your story to make it more likely for you to catch the winds of luck?*

3

Cultivate Courage

Luck favors those who know their limits—
and dare to sail past them.

Are you a risk-taker? Most people instinctively answer with a clear yes or no. The truth, though, is far more nuanced. Risk isn't binary. It comes in many forms.

Consider the wide spectrum of risks, including the social risk of giving a toast at a wedding, the emotional risk of telling someone you love them, the intellectual risk of diving into an unsolved problem, the physical risk of leaping out of a plane with only a parachute, the political risk of sharing an unpopular opinion, or the financial risk of investing in the stock market. Each type of risk tugs at different fears, challenges different parts of your identity, and provokes different levels of excitement or hesitation. You might be fearless in one area and cautious in another. The real question isn't whether you're a risk-taker but rather what kinds of risks you're willing to take in your quest to reach your goals.

What I Wish I Knew About Luck

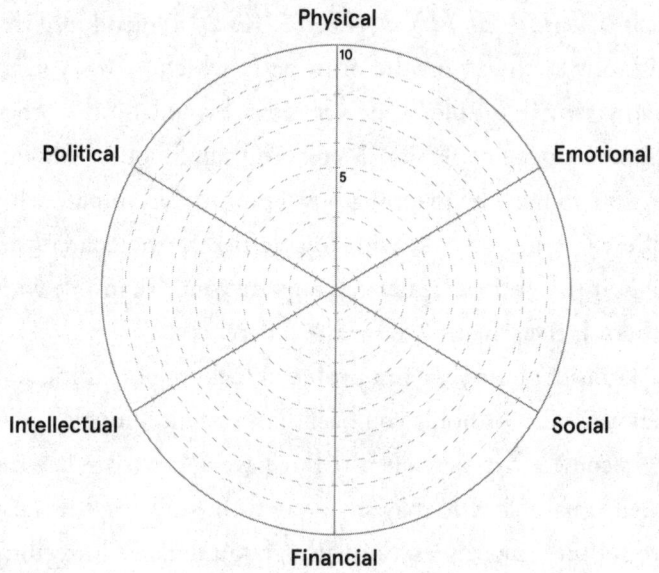

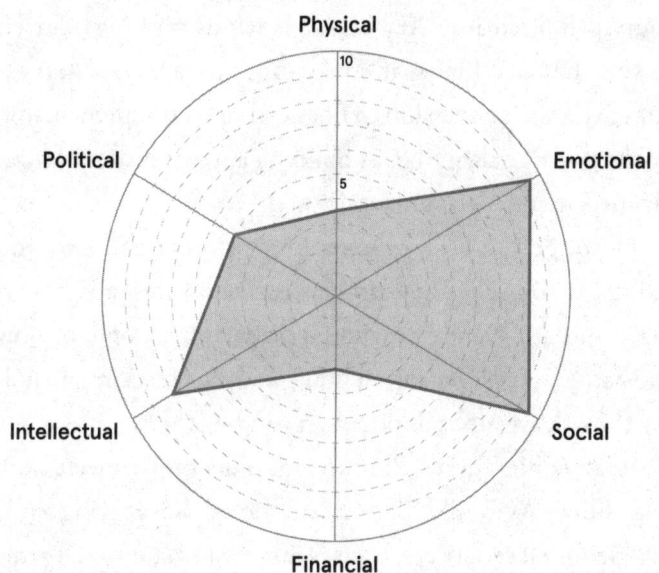

In *What I Wish I Knew When I Was 20*, I introduced the Risk-o-Meter, seen on the prior page, which allows you to map your risk profile.[1] One version is blank, and the other shows my personal Risk-o-Meter. You can fill out the blank version yourself by mapping how comfortable you are with different types of risk, with lowest risk at the center and highest risk at the perimeter. Compare your risk profile with others. It is fascinating to see the differences!

Consider how your risk profile unlocks opportunities for luck to strike, or holds you back. For instance, if you aspire to become a top-tier scientist but have a low tolerance for intellectual risk, you may shy away from studying the most groundbreaking topics. Similarly, if you dream of excelling as a mountain biker but fear getting injured, you might find yourself limited in a sport that demands pushing yourself to your physical limits. If you're eager to launch a start-up but have a strong aversion to financial risk, entrepreneurship might prove challenging, as building a new venture inevitably involves financial uncertainty.

However, risk profiles aren't fixed, just like the story you tell about yourself. They can be stretched if they aren't serving you. Batu Demir provides a powerful example of how you can push past perceived limits and expectations, including the risk aversions imposed on you by others.

From Izmir, Turkey, Batu and his older brother were both born blind. As a child, Batu sat on the sidelines crying while his friends played soccer. He was hungry to get into the game but afraid of getting hurt. Eventually his frustration was greater than his fears, and he committed himself to finding ways that he could participate.

Although he and his brother couldn't see, they had exquisite hearing. So, Batu and his brother slipped a ball into a plastic grocery bag so that the rustle of the plastic alerted them to where the ball moved. At the beginning it was nearly impossible to play this way. Batu fell, he bled, and he broke his arm. But he kept getting up to try again. Batu reflects that "loss is not a door that simply shuts. It is a door that, when closed, forces you to find another way through."

At thirteen, Batu was referred by a friend to a local blind soccer team, and everything changed. Blind soccer is a fast, fiercely competitive sport fueled by skill, strategy, and sound. It's played on a smaller field with sideboards to keep the ball in play; each team fields four blind outfield players and one sighted goalkeeper. Everyone wears eye shades to level the playing field in situations where some players have residual sight. The ball rattles as it rolls, turning acute hearing into a key advantage. When a player moves to challenge an opponent, they shout "Voy!" to announce their presence to keep the play safe and fair. Three sighted guides, including the goalkeeper, the team's primary coach, and another coach behind the goal, shout rapid-fire directions like "You're at ten meters . . . now eight . . . shoot!" Players must constantly tune in, adapt, and act. From the time that Batu discovered blind soccer, it became a central part of his life.

It gave him a sense of freedom, purpose, and joy. On the field, he doesn't feel limited. He feels alive.

Beyond soccer, Batu and his brother also learned to push past perceived limits to ride their bikes around their hometown. They developed a form of echolocation by snapping their fingers and clicking their tongues, listening carefully to the echoes that bounced back to avoid obstacles. Batu acknowledged that they knew their neighborhood well but were sometimes thwarted by cars that would appear out of nowhere. He noted, "You learn quickly when the stakes are high."

These early innovations weren't just fun and games. They taught Batu how to stretch his risk profile and to confront fear through experimentation. He learned that "if a game or a system did not include him, he had the power to rewrite it." He recently traveled the world with his brother with stops in Austria, Hungary, and the Czech Republic; and then he traveled solo to London, the United States, Thailand, Korea, Japan, Singapore, and Hong Kong. Batu is motivated by curiosity and a dream worth chasing. His next destinations are Latin America and Africa.

As he navigates the world, Batu proactively anticipates risks and challenges, and strategizes how to overcome them. He embraces calculated risks, such as stepping onto a random escalator in a train station just to see where it leads. At other times, he patiently waits for fortune to find him in the form of a new train arriving with riders who will help him locate the train station exit. When he graduates from Stanford Graduate School of Business, Batu hopes to channel his ingenuity and determination into a new mission: using technology to make the world more accessible for people with disabilities.

What makes Batu exceptional isn't just his achievements; it's the mindset behind them and his willingness to continue to stretch his risk profile. "Being blind often means I'm either unseen or seen only as a blind person," he reflects. "But I want to be seen for my vision, not just my blindness." Throughout his life he was told that he couldn't do things, such as play soccer, ride bikes, go to the best universities, or contribute to the world. He committed himself to proving others wrong, and to demonstrating that he is not limited. He shared that "normal" is just a construct. "We all experience the world differently," he says. "What are the limits you have accepted without question? And what might be possible if you refused to accept them?"

Batu understands that luck isn't something you wait for but something you prepare for and then act upon. His life is a testament to the idea that when we stretch our risk profiles with purpose, we don't just navigate the world differently; we expand what's possible.

Luck emerges as a direct by-product of stretching beyond your comfort zone because it expands your "luck surface area," a concept introduced by Jim Collins in *Great by Choice*.[2] Collins defines the luck surface area as the extent to which a person or organization is exposed to opportunities. The larger the surface area—that is, the larger your sail—the greater your chances of encountering good luck.

Keep in mind that not all risks are created equal. Some might lead to minor embarrassment, while others can be life-threatening. That's why it's essential to know yourself and your capabilities well enough to minimize the downside. For instance, it will likely be nerve-racking to give an impromptu speech if public speaking terrifies you, but it is reckless to hop on a motorcycle without knowing how to ride. The key is distinguishing between perceived and actual danger: a snake bite is truly hazardous; giving a toast at a wedding is not. Smart risk-takers also work to reduce risk before stepping up. Athletes train to lower physical risk, musicians rehearse to reduce social risks, investors perform due diligence to mitigate financial risks, and scientists review the literature to lower intellectual risks.

Also, some types of risk are likely irreversible, such as quitting your job. Some are clearly reversible, such as trying a new hobby. Jeff Bezos, the founder of Amazon, describes these as one-way door decisions and two-way door decisions, respectively.[3] Since one-way decisions are very difficult to undo, it behooves you to take your time when making those decisions. Since two-way door decisions are easier to unwind, you can take less time agonizing over them and instead view them as experiments.

Another way to evaluate what risks you can and can't afford is to look at the consequences of different types of errors. Type I errors are false positives that happen when you find something that isn't there. For example, telling someone they have an illness when they really don't. Type II errors are false negatives that occur when you miss something. For example, failing to detect when someone has a disease. Imagine a fire alarm going off when there's no fire. That's annoying but not dangerous (Type I error). Now imagine a fire breaking out but the alarm stays silent. That could be disastrous (Type II error)!

In many cases, a false positive isn't a huge problem. If a medical test mistakenly says someone has an illness, they might just need a second test to confirm. But missing a real illness could mean not getting life-saving treatment in time. That's why medical tests are often designed to catch as many real cases as possible, even if it means sometimes raising false alarms.

In another example, if someone is using a dating app, a Type I error would result in a date with someone you don't like (a false positive), while a Type II error would entail passing on going on a date with someone who could have been a great match (a false negative). In both cases the goal is to strike the right balance between risks and rewards based on what's at stake and what you can afford to lose.

Sometimes no matter what options are available, you might lean toward risk aversion. I will never be a big physical or financial risk-taker. However, that doesn't mean I won't encounter physical and financial challenges that need to be addressed. The key is to find partners with complementary risk profiles. My husband, for instance, never met a ladder he didn't want to climb. Whenever there is a problem at our house that requires getting up on the roof—say, to clear the gutters—Michael gets out the thirty-foot extension ladder and zips up. It is no big deal to him, and just the thought of it makes me queasy. Knowing that I have a partner with a complementary risk profile allows me to live in and maintain a house that otherwise would fall into disrepair.

Knowing your risk profile informs what types of challenges you're willing to take on, where you need to stretch, and where you need assistance. Since good luck often lurks just outside your current comfort zone, it behooves you to stretch when possible.

- *What is your risk profile?*
- *How might your risk profile hold you back from attaining your goals?*
- *What risks do you need to take to see and seize more luck?*

4

Expand Your Sail

*Luck favors those who develop abilities
that increase the size of their sail.*

Barkotel Zemenu was fortunate to grow up in Addis
Ababa, the capital of Ethiopia, with an older sister who
was in the midst of applying to college just before he entered
high school. Watching her navigate the process gave him a
glimpse into a world of possibilities beyond his own. At the
time, however, those possibilities felt far out of reach.

Barkotel spoke primarily Amharic, one of Ethiopia's languages, and his English was rudimentary at best. This was
a major barrier to pursuing higher education in the United
States. Undeterred, Barkotel turned this obstacle into a challenge. Beginning in ninth grade, he committed to learning
five new English words each day.

Five words a day may seem modest, but over time Barkotel's knowledge compounded. Slowly his vocabulary expanded to the point where he could read more complicated

texts in English. He set a bold goal: to read the entire Sherlock Holmes series, looking up every unfamiliar word as he went. By the time it came for him to apply for college, not only had Barkotel amassed an impressive vocabulary but he also opened a door that was once closed. With his strong academic record and his persistence in learning English, he gained admission to Yale.

Once at Yale, Barkotel had to meet the university's requirement to study a second language. This time he chose Hebrew, driven by a desire to read the Hebrew Bible in its original language. He tackled this task with the same determination he had used to master English, listening to Hebrew audio recordings as he walked across campus even before he could distinguish individual words, and he sat at dedicated Hebrew-speaking tables over meals at school so that he was immersed in the language for a good part of the day. It worked.

After mastering Hebrew, Barkotel set his sights on Chinese. Again, his disciplined approach led to fluency. He even read me a poem he wrote to his Chinese teacher at the end of his first semester. The poem made his teacher cry.... Next came Greek, and then Arabic.

Each time Barkotel picked up a new language, friends would teasingly ask if he was in love with someone who spoke that language. The answer was always no; he was simply in love with languages. This skill would never have developed unless Barkotel started his journey into English with five new words a day. He would never have known that he had a talent for learning languages unless he tried.

This skill is now a vital part of Barkotel's ship, opening the door to opportunities that he would never be able to seize if he didn't speak all these languages. As a doctoral student studying dark matter in the universe, Barkotel was able to do research abroad at the Weizmann Institute of Science, a premier astrophysical institute in Israel where most of the work communication happened in Hebrew. This opportunity gave him the rare chance to operate telescopes in the Negev desert while soaking in an environment that he had only heard of secondhand. And having sufficient expertise in Chinese enabled Barkotel to teach in rural China, where he taught eleventh-grade Chinese students about dark matter in their native language.

This is consistent with the journalist and author Malcolm Gladwell's argument in *Outliers*[1] that raw talent alone is not enough to be successful. You must be willing and able to persist to truly master a new skill. Gladwell examined research by Anders Ericsson[2] showing that to become an expert in a complex skill such as music, sports, or chess requires about ten thousand hours of deliberate practice. This assessment came after analyzing case studies of successful individuals and groups, such as the Beatles, who played thousands of hours in Hamburg before becoming famous, and Bill Gates, who had early access to computers and spent extensive amounts of time programming as a teenager. Not surprisingly, the more you practice, the better you get and the more successful you will become.

Skills and talents are key components of your ship because they open doors to opportunities that wouldn't exist if you didn't have them. But how do you know what talents to pursue? We aren't born with a list of what we can or will do best. Barkotel wouldn't have known that he had a natural talent for learning languages unless he tried and put in the hours of effort.

In fact, we are sometimes dissuaded from pursuing certain paths simply because we don't show immediate talent or those fields aren't culturally encouraged or valued. As a result, we each need to face the challenge of deciding which skills and talents to nurture. This brings us to the age-old question: Should you double down on your strengths or focus on strengthening your weaknesses? The answer is rarely obvious. You often won't know where your true strengths lie until you invest time and effort and are motivated enough to persist through the early stages of struggle. Talent often reveals itself through consistent practice, not just at the starting line. What may initially seem like a weakness could, with time and effort, evolve into an area of unexpected strength. The real art is to remain curious and open long enough to discover which pursuits spark your aptitude and passion.

Since few of us are naturally good at everything, part of growing into your potential involves deciding which skills you want to strengthen. If you love music, should you pursue a singing career even if you can't carry a tune? If you're fascinated by medicine, should you become a surgeon if you faint at the sight of blood? Or should you instead steer toward paths that feel more natural from the outset? The key is self-awareness: being honest about where you are willing to struggle, where you are eager to grow, and where your natural talents give you a running start.

Those who are lucky in life find pursuits that resonate with their natural talents and passions. Tom Rath studied the role of natural talents in *StrengthsFinder 2.0*. He writes, "While it may be possible, with a considerable amount of work, to add talent where little exists, our research suggests that this may not be the best use of your time." He continues, "Instead, we've discovered that the most successful people start with dominant talent—and then add skills, knowledge, and practice to the mix. When they do this, the raw talent serves as a multiplier. Talent x Investment = Strength."[3]

Success is, therefore, the direct result of your natural talents, motivation, and behavior. However, finding a great match for your talents doesn't always happen early. That was certainly the case for me. When I graduated with a PhD in neuroscience, I knew that I didn't want to continue as a lab scientist. I loved science, learning, teaching, and writing, but the day-to-day life of a bench scientist was not for me. As a result, I literally changed careers every two years for over a decade, from working at the San Jose Technology Museum, now called The Tech, as an exhibit designer, to consulting for Fortune 500 companies as a management consultant, to writing children's science books, to starting a multimedia company, all in pursuit of a match. When I started each new role, I fully intended to spend my entire career there learning and growing my depth of knowledge and expertise. But there was always something missing or not just right. It wasn't until I was forty years old that I ended up in a role that truly complemented my skills and interests. That's when the winds of luck picked up and I was ready to catch them by hoisting my sail high!

Here's the way it happened. It was 1999, and I saw a job posting about building the new entrepreneurship center at Stanford University School of Engineering, and I was intrigued. The job was very junior, and I was reluctant to consider it, initially crumpling up the job description that I had printed out and throwing it in the trash. However, I listened to my gut and pulled it out of the trash the next day. After applying, I had eleven interviews and was ultimately offered the position. It soon became clear that I was finally in the right place, and I was quickly rewarded with more responsibilities and opportunities.

After having the good fortune to see the job listing and take a chance by applying, I entered a jet stream of good luck because I applied my talents and skills with laser focus. Importantly, what I had learned in my prior roles contributed greatly to my toolbox of skills. I hadn't wasted time in the circuitous path to a career I loved; rather, everything I learned was additive. Working on the team designing exhibits for

The Tech taught me how to imagine a future that didn't yet exist. Working as a management consultant taught me critical lessons about developing strategies. Starting a multimedia company prepared me to build a team with a wide array of skills and interests.

Sometimes those with latent talent don't find their way to a role that is a match for them. Imagine what would have happened if the Beatles had never picked up musical instruments or if Bill Gates hadn't had access as a teenager to a computer? "The real tragedy of life," says Rath, "is not that each of us doesn't have enough strengths, it's that we fail to use the ones we have."

Having a mentor to help you identify your talents can be a life-changing experience. About twenty years ago, I had a colleague who was really struggling at work. Each week he and I had a hard conversation about assignments that were not going well, and I did my best to coach him on how to improve. Unfortunately, it wasn't working. Despite his desire, the job was just not tuned to his skills. He could have kept trying, but success was not in the cards. So, I spent time thinking about what he did well, and it became clear to me that he would be a fabulous salesperson. He was strikingly personable and engaging, and he was a terrific communicator. When I suggested this to him, he was aghast. He hadn't remotely considered a sales career and, even more, he had a strong negative impression of what it meant to be in sales.

Yet he didn't dismiss the idea entirely. After leaving his role in our organization, he explored sales opportunities and ultimately took a position at a large company. Almost immediately his career took off, and within a short time he was responsible for launching and leading the company's sales office in a new country! To this day his sales career continues to blossom. We stay in touch, and it is a joy to see him thriving. This story is a potent reminder of the importance of finding yourself in a place that truly resonates with your natural talents. Once that happens, the winds of luck begin to blow with gusto.

For those, like me, who didn't immediately find a match between their talents and their role, it is important to remember that passions follow engagement, not the other way around. You will never know what you're passionate about or what you're skilled at unless you experiment. Barkotel is proof that passions are the result of exposure and experience. He might never have learned of his talents and passion for languages unless he started with five new words a day. The key is to try lots of things, see what sticks, and watch as the winds pick up!

This begs the question of how to deal with your weaknesses. Small weaknesses are like holes in your sail, and larger weaknesses are like holes in your ship. They diminish your effectiveness and may even sink your ability to reach your goals. You need to be honest with yourself about your shortcomings and find ways to compensate. You can patch holes by learning skills that need improvement, or you can find team members to complement your weaknesses. The best teams have people with diverse skills and interests who can fill in the gaps for one another. The key is self-awareness: You need to know when to double down on what you do best, when to challenge yourself to grow in areas that could unlock new doors, and when to partner with others who complement your skills. This resonates with the ideas in the last chapter where I discussed working with those with complementary risk profiles.

The best teams with whom I've worked aren't just a collection of talented individuals but an ensemble with diverse and unique skills and interests. For example, a strategist needs an organized executor, and a creative powerhouse needs a logistician who will find all the places where an innovative idea might fail. It's this interplay of diverse perspectives that allows individuals and teams to navigate complex situations, solve problems more effectively, and address opportunities that might otherwise be missed. By intentionally identifying and then honing your own skills, and cultivating relationships with those who think differently, you build a stronger ship and are positioned to catch the winds of luck as they blow by.

- *What are your strengths and weaknesses?*
- *How will you play to your strengths to catch more luck?*
- *Can you find others with complementary strengths to balance your weaknesses?*

5

Set Your North Star

Luck favors those with clear goals, pointing them toward their objectives.

At sixteen, Sonia Garcia lost her father to suicide. From that day on, she knew she wanted to dedicate her life to supporting people living with mental illness and the families who love them. Along with her cofounder, Stas Sokolin, who had relevant personal experiences, Sonia started Amae Health, a company that creates tailored clinical and compassionate support for those suffering with mental illness.

In their very first conversation, Sonia and Stas realized they shared something rare: They had witnessed firsthand how broken the system can be for individuals with severe mental health challenges. They didn't see anyone else building what they knew was needed, so they said, "If not us, then who?" From that sense of urgency and shared experience, Amae Health was born.[1]

They named the company Amae, inspired by a Japanese concept that speaks to our innate need for connection and the ability to depend on others to rebuild, heal, and grow stronger. At its core, *amae* is about the essential role of community in helping us find our way back when we've been brought to our knees; a reminder that none of us are meant to do this alone.

When asked what advice she would give to others facing a moment of upheaval, Sonia said, "I've known since the day I lost my father to suicide, when I was just sixteen, that this was my purpose. That moment changed everything." She advises others that "if you're faced with a moment of loss or inspiration that stirs something in you, lean into it. Let it shape you. Let it guide you. And once you've found that sense of purpose, pursue it relentlessly."

Sometimes a clear direction—a North Star—reveals itself with striking clarity. This often happens in response to a discontinuity in your life, a moment that breaks the rhythm of the ordinary and demands your attention. A profound personal loss or a life-altering failure can shift your entire perspective, stripping away distractions and clarifying what truly matters, as it did for Sonia. It might also be something unexpectedly beautiful, like hearing a violin concerto that stirs something deep within you, awakening a passion you didn't know you had. In that instant, a path unfolds, illuminated by a sense of purpose or possibility. Whether born from adversity or inspiration, these moments reframe your relationship with the world and offer a direction that feels less like a choice and more like a calling.

The researchers Edwin A. Locke and Gary P. Latham share a thirty-five-year retrospective study on the role of purpose and goal setting in their paper "Building a Practically Useful Theory of Goal Setting and Task Motivation: A 35 Year Odyssey."[2] They found that simply deciding to "do your best" rarely leads to successful outcomes. Instead, it is much more helpful to set very clear, challenging goals that point you in a specific direction. Goals stimulate increased effort, push you further, help you maintain momentum in the face of inevitable obstacles, and encourage you to come up with innovative maneuvers around those obstacles on the way to your goals.

They emphasize that successful goal setting is not just about choosing an objective but fully committing to it with sincerity and persistence. Achieving meaningful goals requires regularly assessing whether you are on track, making necessary adjustments, and maintaining a deep belief in your ability to reach your desired destination. Without this belief, motivation can wane, and setbacks may feel insurmountable.

In my classes, I ask students to create their own Professional Happiness Designs—PHDs—to help codify their short-term and long-term goals. The act of formally setting your North Star by noting where you are now, where you want to go, and how you plan to get there is a meaningful exercise, and one that we rarely take the time to do. This exercise needs to be repeated every few years, since our goals inevitably change in response to our life circumstances. One of the most valuable outcomes of this exercise is that the students get to see the PHDs of their classmates, some of whom have very clear short-term goals such as graduating and getting a job, while others have mapped a less defined path to a large world stage. There is certainly no value judgment, since we all get to choose the stage on which we play out our lives. Sometimes, however, seeing others' goals helps students adjust their own, stretching further than they originally imagined.

Anson Zhou, a medical student, shared with me his unique practice: He writes letters to himself that articulate his short-term ambitions and goals. Written from the perspective of his future self, as if he has already achieved them. In these letters he might write statements such as "I started medical school" or "I accepted a job at a medtech company." Some goals are already in motion and likely to come to fruition, while others are purely aspirational. On his computer, goals that haven't yet been achieved are written in blue, while those that have appear in black. This color-coding system allows Anson to periodically review the letters, reminding himself of his aspirations and focusing his intention on the dreams still ahead. When he achieves a goal, no matter how long it takes, he triumphantly changes the text from blue to black. Once an entire letter contains no more blue text, he writes a new letter filled with fresh aspirations. By setting his intentions in this way, Anson transforms his long-term visions into specific short-term goals, which he then breaks down into concrete actions. For instance, his goal of attending medical school led him to schedule time for application essays and to reach out to his cousin for interview practice.

Luck favors those who are clear about where they're headed and committed to showing up for the journey. When you have a specific objective in mind, something powerful happens: your attention sharpens, your decisions become more intentional, and you notice opportunities that might have otherwise passed you by. It's like adjusting the focus on a camera. What once looked blurry suddenly comes into focus. The world hasn't changed, but your place in it has. When I am writing a book, for example, my attention is intensely tuned to stories that fit the theme. My eyes and ears are wide open to relevant examples that I can use in the book. Anson's story is a prime example.

For particularly complex or ambitious goals, roadblocks are inevitable. There will be false starts, mistakes, and even outright failures along the way. Rather than viewing these as signs of defeat, it is crucial to reframe them as opportunities for growth and learning. Each obstacle presents valuable insights that can refine your approach and strengthen your resilience. True success is measured not only by steady progress toward the goal but also by the personal and strategic growth that happens throughout the journey. The ability to navigate these difficulties and maintain forward momentum despite setbacks is a key aspect of resilience. These skills are discussed in more depth in chapter 15, which focuses specifically on resilience and the role it plays in long-term success.

Remember, life isn't a sprint, it's a marathon, and each mile will have different priorities. Trying to juggle everything at the same time can lead to burnout and frustration. Therefore, take time to reflect on which priorities deserve the spotlight right now and what truly needs your attention. This kind of clarity helps you filter out noise, recognize relevant connections, and respond decisively when doors open. When your mind is primed to see the potential, you're more likely to strike up a conversation with someone with a shared interest, ask questions that help you address a relevant problem, and say yes to the opportunity that moves you closer to your goals. Serendipity begins to feel less random and more like a natural by-product of your focus.

As the Cheshire Cat famously told Alice in *Alice's Adventures in Wonderland*, "If you don't know where you're going, any road will get you there." Sometimes that mindset can be liberating, as it invites you to embrace the unexpected and uncover opportunities you couldn't have planned for. But other times, having a clear destination is essential. Like navigating at sea, life calls for different strategies to catch the winds of luck. At times, it's wise to drift and explore; at others, you must steer with intention toward a defined goal. The key is knowing when to surrender to the wind and when to take the helm. That's why it helps to carry a compass, your personal North Star, to keep you oriented even as the winds shift.

Specificity fuels momentum, so the clearer you are about what you want, the easier it becomes to channel your time, energy, and relationships toward making it real. Vague hopes rarely lead to concrete outcomes. When your goals are defined, they act like beacons illuminating the path forward and helping you find opportunities that resonate with your objectives.

- *What is your North Star?*
- *Where are you now?*
- *Where do you want to go?*
- *How will you get there?*

Part 2

Recruit Your Crew

Luck seldom sails solo.

—Tina Seelig

6

Ask for Luck

*Luck favors those who know what they
want and ask for it clearly.*

When Bhav Jain was in high school, he was eager to get involved in scientific research, but there wasn't a clear path to pursue this through his school. Lacking any formal experience or credentials, he relied on the two things he did have: curiosity and drive. He wrote letters to hundreds of faculty members at multiple local universities in Pittsburgh, Pennsylvania, casting a wide net across various fields. The response rate was very low; only about 2 percent of the professors wrote back. Although initially discouraged, he realized that this 2 percent was enough! He exchanged messages with each of those who responded and dug deeper into their research interests. Impressed, one of the professors offered Bhav the chance to work in his lab.

Bhav continued this approach when he went off to college, where he again leaned on his letter-writing strategy. He sent hundreds of emails to faculty at universities around the country. He asked highly specific questions of each of the recipients. This targeted approach, combined with the credibility he built as an MIT student, dramatically increased his success rate. Now, about 40 percent of the recipients responded. Some of those exchanges evolved into collaborations and culminated in published articles.

Today, as a medical student at Stanford, Bhav continues to apply the strategy. With his accumulated experience, the response rate has soared to an astonishing 95 percent, and he now mentors those who reach out to him for guidance.

Bhav's journey demonstrates that opportunities don't simply appear. You must reach for them. Early attempts may yield few results, but just one response can result in a ripple effect of follow-up opportunities. Bhav was able to make a couple of contacts in high school, which resulted in opportunities that helped him land in a terrific university. From there, he made more contacts and created even more opportunities, and so on. You might look at Bhav now and say he is so lucky, and you would be right. But it all started by asking for what he wanted again and again.

Asking for what you want early in life is one of the best strategies for getting what you want. Sometimes you need to literally knock on doors. My husband, Michael, graduated in the middle of a recession in 1983, and jobs were scarce, especially for someone who was trying to change fields from political science to technology marketing. So, what did he do? He drove around Silicon Valley and knocked on doors—real doors. He went to dozens of companies each day asking if they were hiring, as opposed to combing through the want ads in the newspaper and blindly sending in his résumé. He knew that his résumé would never make it through the initial screening since his formal experiences didn't match what he wanted to do. After many months, this strategy eventually paid off when he met the president of a small company who happened to be in the lobby when Michael walked in the door. They had a conversation about Michael's interests and the company's needs, and he was hired into a junior marketing role. This launched Michael's career in Silicon Valley. How lucky! That luck would never have materialized if he hadn't tirelessly asked for what he wanted.

This strategy is also helpful later in your career, when you are already established. Mariano-Florentino Cuéllar, known as Tino, is a former justice of the Supreme Court of California and the current president of the Carnegie Endowment for International Peace. Much of his success comes from reaching out to those who appear to have similar interests and goals to find synergies in their work. When Tino saw an editorial about artificial intelligence in *The New York Times*, he reached out to the author, whom he didn't know, sharing his interest in this topic. Their conversations continued over several months, and they eventually worked together in launching a nonprofit to map the impact of AI, including technology trends, risks, and benefits for society. This never would have happened if he hadn't taken a risk and reached out with a cold email. Tino's approach exemplifies the invisible effort behind so many successful people. They don't just wait for opportunities to appear; they actively seek them out.

It's not just that you ask but how you do it. It's important to frame your requests in a way that sparks interest, aligns with the motivations of the person you are contacting, and makes it easy for them to say yes. Requests for help are essentially a story, and the better your story resonates with the recipient, the more likely the other person is to respond. Whether it's a quick introduction or a piece of advice, the best initial requests make it easy for the recipient to extend a helping hand.

The organizational psychologist Adam Grant coined the term "five-minute favor" to describe small, low-effort acts of generosity that can deliver significant value to the recipient while requiring minimal effort from the giver. He introduced this concept in *Give and Take*,[1] his book in which he explores the power of generosity in creating networks of trust and opportunity. The idea is simple: When you ask for a small favor, such as a quick introduction, feedback on an idea, or help answering a specific question, your request is more likely to be granted than if you asked for something more time-consuming or burdensome.

What makes the five-minute favor so effective is its asymmetrical impact. A moment of someone's time can unlock massive value for the person doing the asking. It might open a door, validate a concept, or connect you with someone who can change the trajectory of your work or life. Meanwhile, for the giver, the effort is often so negligible that they might not even remember it the next day.

Piya Sorcar is masterful at asking for five-minute favors, resulting in waves of increasing engagement from others who are ultimately inspired to rally behind her vision. As the founder of TeachAids, she has raised millions of dollars and enlisted dozens of celebrities as voice actors for her educational software. How did she pull this off? By relentlessly asking for small favors.

Piya was on a mission to equip young people around the world, especially in India, with life-saving knowledge about HIV prevention. Educational materials on the topic were scarce, fueling a growing epidemic. But she refused to let that stand in her way. She shared her passion with everyone she met. One day, while telling a friend about her work and her hope to find a high-profile actor in India to provide an endorsement for this project, she learned that her friend's uncle, an eye doctor in India, treated a legendary Indian actor. The friend suggested that maybe he could introduce Piya. Most people would have nodded politely and moved on, since this felt so random. But Piya did the opposite! She seized the opportunity and followed up by asking for a five-minute favor from this actor, communicated through his eye doctor. She was surprised and delighted to be offered a brief meeting with the actor while he was between takes on a movie set in India.

With no guarantee of success in engaging the actor in her cause, Piya dug into her savings and bought a plane ticket to India. When she arrived, she was given exactly five minutes with the movie actor. She made her pitch. He listened. Then instead of dismissing her, he asked her to wait while he shot another scene. When he returned, he wanted to hear more.

After a few more five-minute conversations, the actor surprised Piya with his next comment: "You need to meet my wife." Confused, Piya asked why. As it turned out, his wife, another famous actor, was also a passionate social activist. That very week his wife had been embroiled in a public debate about whether HIV-positive children should be allowed to attend school, and she was desperate for credible educational materials to help inform the public. Piya had exactly what she needed, and at that moment, everything clicked. The actor and his wife not only agreed to lend their voices to TeachAids but also joined as advisors. How lucky! Of course, Piya was lucky, but that luck came from creating the teaching materials, telling everyone about her work, and asking for five-minute favors that got her closer to her goals.

No one knows how to help you unless you tell them what you need. And more often than not, you will find people who are willing and even eager to help if you give them the chance. There are a few things, however, to keep in mind when asking others for help.

First, beware of "favor fatigue," which arises from asking lots of favors from the same person. One or two favors are fine, but then it is out of line, unless you have a relationship with that person and they, too, are asking you for favors. Don't treat your friends or colleagues like vending machines who can be approached for a quick favor any time. Consider each favor you ask carefully, thinking about how you phrase it, how much you are asking of the person on the other end, and how you are expressing appreciation even before the favor is granted.

Second, clarity is key when making a request. One of the worst ways to ask is with a request to "pick your brain." These requests usually lack any clear direction, leaving the recipient to decipher what you need and whether they can realistically help you within a reasonable timeframe. Beyond the ambiguity, there's often an unintentional sense of entitlement in the phrasing that focuses solely on what you want without considering the recipient's time or perspective. A well-structured, thoughtful request, on the other hand, increases the chances of a productive and mutually beneficial exchange. For example, "I'd welcome a chance to ask you a few questions, either in person or via email." Keep in mind that the goal of the first connection is usually to get to the next one. So small, clear requests make the most sense.

Third, do your homework. Learn about the person's experiences, read articles they have written, or watch talks they have given. Understand what's important to them, personally and professionally. This level of preparation not only demonstrates respect for their work and their time but also equips you with information that can make your interaction more meaningful. Also, by doing your homework, you can ask questions that are beyond what is already publicly available. You might also discover shared interests, be it a love of surfing, a fascination with Stoicism, or a passion for molecular gastronomy. These points of connection can serve as natural conversation starters, helping to build rapport and establish common ground. People tend to engage more deeply when they feel understood, and showing that you've taken the time to learn about their perspectives creates a foundation of trust and mutual interest.

Fourth, make yourself easy to help. I learned this from my friend and colleague Heidi Roizen, a venture capitalist who receives countless requests for guidance and introductions. Her advice is simple: If you want her to make an introduction, make it effortless for her. Provide a short, prewritten email that she can easily forward. This should include a concise, thoughtful introduction of yourself and a clear explanation of why you want to connect with that person specifically. By doing this, you remove the burden of crafting the message from the person helping you, making it far more likely they'll follow through. The key to making it easy for someone to do you a five-minute favor is to turn it into a one-minute favor. When you lower the effort required, you significantly increase the chances of getting the help you need.

Fifth, ask how you can help them. Instead of assuming that favors are a one-way street, ask if perhaps there is something that you can do to help them. Finding ways to reciprocate is a powerful way to build a real relationship. Examples include offering to help them with a project, sending articles that might be of interest, or volunteering to amplify their work. Take time to think about the resources you have that might be valuable and the opportunities you can put in front of them in exchange for the help they are providing. Heidi shared a story about someone who wanted some career coaching. She was extremely busy and was heading out of town for a conference, so the person offered to drive her to the airport. They talked all the way. This was a clever win-win solution.

Sixth, always follow through with your commitments. If you agree to meet at a specific time, then show up on time. If you offer to send relevant information, do it! These small actions demonstrate respect for the other person's time and help to build trust. Consistency in keeping your commitments also sets the tone for future interactions. When you're dependable, others are more likely to trust you with future opportunities. Reliability is the glue that holds relationships together. Failing to follow through in a timely manner, even on seemingly minor commitments, can have lasting consequences. Remember, also, that when someone introduces you to someone else, your behavior is a reflection on them. When you don't deliver on what you promised, you send an implicit message that your words don't carry weight. You break the chain of trust, and it is unlikely you will get a response in the future.

Finally, remember that everything someone does for you is a gift, an investment of their time, energy, and goodwill. Whenever someone takes the time to help you, whether by offering advice, making an introduction, or sharing their experiences, they are taking time away from something else. A heartfelt thank-you goes a long way, as discussed in the following chapter. This small act of acknowledgment sets you apart because, surprisingly, so many people fail to do it. In a world where many are quick to ask but slow to appreciate, those who genuinely express thanks stand out. And that can be a powerful advantage, unlocking lucky breaks.

Take the time to figure out what you need, who might be able to help you, and make short actionable requests that are likely to resonate with the recipients. Of course, you won't always score a goal. You don't need everyone to say yes. You only need one response to start a chain reaction that can lead to something much bigger. Luck favors those who are both clear in their intentions and bold enough to ask.

- *What do you need?*
- *Who will you ask?*
- *How will you ask, such that it is likely to get a lucky response?*

7

Appreciate Luck

Luck favors those who give thanks—
goodwill grows into good fortune.

W hat experiments could you perform to determine how different parts of the brain work?"

This is a homework assignment that Dr. Jerome Schwartzbaum gave our class during my second year of college. My mind started swimming. This was the first time I had received an assignment like this, demonstrating that I had finally reached the frontier of what we know and that I could possibly cross that frontier.

I went home and wrote and wrote and wrote, outlining a long list of potential experiments that could be performed. A week later, I received my paper back, and on the top it said, "Tina, you think like a scientist." At that moment I became a scientist! The words propelled me forward as nothing else had before. The feeling was positively exhilarating. I shared this story in *What I Wish I Knew When I Was 20* as an example of how other people shape how we think about our place in the world.

Fast-forward twenty years to when I began teaching entrepreneurship at Stanford and frequently thought about how the encouraging comments given to me by Dr. Schwartzbaum so many years earlier had changed my life. I picked up a pen and paper and wrote him a thank-you note acknowledging how much he influenced me and my teaching. My letter, sent via US post to the university, may or may not have reached him since I never heard back. In fact, I didn't even know if he was still alive.

Another twenty years passed. . . . Out of the blue, I received an email from Dr. Schwartzbaums's granddaughter. She wrote to tell me that her grandfather had recently passed away at ninety-five years old. Her note said that her father had shared an excerpt of my letter at her grandfather's funeral. She wrote, "On behalf of my whole family, thank you for your kind words about my grandfather. We are so grateful that he is able to live on through his students, especially fellow scientists and educators like yourself." Her words touched my heart as I realized that my words of appreciation, written twenty years earlier in response to his words to me twenty years before that, had been passed on through two generations. It demonstrated that a single gesture, no matter how small, can ripple across time and touch the lives of people we don't know in ways we may never fully understand.

Appreciation is one of the most underrated ways to boost

your luck. A simple sincere act of kindness, acknowledging someone's efforts on your behalf, can have outsize effects. It strengthens relationships, reinforces goodwill, and keeps you top of mind. Over time, these small gestures expand your sail, making it more likely to catch the next gust of good fortune. When new opportunities arise, they are often extended to those who have shown genuine appreciation in the past.

There are two parts to the gratitude-appreciation equation:

- **Gratitude**, in which you *acknowledge to yourself* that something good has happened to you
- **Appreciation**, in which you *demonstrate* your gratitude to the responsible person

There is considerable research on the value of gratitude, which is shown to boost your energy, help you stay focused, and even make you feel more motivated. People who practice gratitude often feel less stressed, more purposeful, and more resilient when facing challenges. Gratitude also strengthens relationships, builds self-confidence, and encourages kindness and generosity.[1] On a biological level, gratitude lights up the brain's reward system and triggers the release of oxytocin, the same hormone that helps us feel trust and connection with others.[2] A review of sixty-four studies about gratitude shows that it also results in a more positive mood and emotions overall.[3] This is why keeping a gratitude journal is such a positive habit, ending each day with a list of all the things for which you are grateful. This habit has been shown to improve mental health with daily practice.[4]

Appreciation, the act of actually expressing your gratitude, compounds these effects. Making the time and effort to demonstrate gratitude significantly strengthens relationships. Appreciation within teams, for example, results in better collaboration, a greater willingness to share ideas, and a generally positive attitude toward work. These benefits are seen in personal relationships, too. In marriages, consistently showing appreciation reduces stress and leads to more resilient relationships, able to weather the storms of daily life.[5]

Showing appreciation is also contagious. When you show appreciation, it is much more likely that others will show appreciation too, creating a gratitude loop. And, as an added benefit, showing appreciation also affects those who witness it. Research shows that people are positively disposed toward working with those who express appreciation to others because they notice and acknowledge those who contribute.[6] Expressing appreciation, therefore, has both direct and indirect benefits and makes everyone better off.

The benefits also extend to employee retention. Evidence shows that employees who receive words of appreciation for their work are much less likely to quit. A terrific example comes from the Campbell Soup Company, which was failing early in the century. The company made a dramatic turnaround between 2001 and 2010, when Douglas Conant took over as CEO. He set as one of his goals to make everyone in the company feel appreciated. He accomplished this in part by writing thank-you notes, a total of more than thirty thousand during his ten-year tenure. That's an average of ten per day! Writing thank-you notes forces you to reflect on the accomplishments of others, giving you a greater appreciation of the work they've done, and it gives the recipient reinforcement for a job well done.[7] In part because of this effort, by the end of the decade, the company had returned to its place as one of the top performing food companies.[8]

I have developed a related practice of writing thank-you notes every night. After reviewing my schedule, I send notes to all those who helped me that day. It might be those who spoke in my class, those who did a particularly effective job executing an event, or those who met with me to discuss a project. As a result, at the end of each day, I feel tremendous gratitude and express my appreciation to each of them.

Sadly, people often underestimate the power of a simple expression of appreciation and miss the chance to offer it. Showing appreciation isn't just a matter of good manners; it's also strategic. Those who express genuine thanks are far more likely to receive help again in the future, while those who don't may find their next request quietly declined. I wish I had understood this earlier in my career when I was more often on the receiving end of favors. Now that I'm more likely the one being asked for help, I appreciate that every favor, whether freely given or part of someone's job, is still a choice.

Acknowledging it shows respect and makes the giver more likely to agree to future favors.

Remember, you can even show appreciation when things don't turn out as you had hoped. This demonstrates an even greater depth of gratitude, since the receiver must mine the experience for value. I ran an entrepreneurship fellowship program for twenty years at the Stanford Technology Ventures Program (STVP), and acceptance rates were quite low. When applicants weren't accepted, it was usual for them to feel disappointed. Sometimes those who didn't get in sent a follow-up message to me. In some cases, they asked what they could have done better. In some cases, they complained about the outcome. In rare cases, they sent a note thanking us for the chance to apply.

Several years ago I received a very kind note from an applicant, Brian, who had been rejected from the program twice. I was so moved by his gracious note that I invited him to meet with me. Our conversation covered lots of topics, including his interest in different styles of leadership based on his experience on the Stanford football team. We ended up crafting an independent study project for him the following academic quarter in which he studied how leadership approaches used during athletic training could be applied in different educational settings.

Brian and I met several times throughout the quarter to discuss his progress. After completing his project, he was inspired to turn his ideas into the nonprofit organization, called Play for Tomorrow, which applies football training techniques to help young people from disadvantaged backgrounds excel in school. He launched and expanded the program, running it for several years and positively impacting hundreds of young people through his knowledge, skills, and uplifting attitude.

His thank-you note became the catalyst for many waves of good luck, ones that Brian acknowledges would not have materialized otherwise. He caught the winds of luck, though it didn't blow in the direction he initially envisioned when he applied to the fellowship program. By reframing his disappointment into a learning experience, he transformed a setback into a springboard for something completely different.

The value of showing appreciation runs deep in our evolutionary roots. Among primates, grooming serves a purpose far beyond hygiene. It's a powerful social ritual, remarkably akin to how humans express appreciation. Biologists and anthropologists have long noted that grooming is a form of emotional currency. Apes and monkeys often groom those who have helped them in the past and those whose support they may need in the future as a kind of social investment, as a way of saying thank you. This mutual exchange strengthens bonds, fosters trust, and maintains the cohesion of the group. Grooming is frequently traded for other vital favors, such as protection, food, or backup in conflict, making it not just an act of appreciation but a strategic tool for navigating complex relationships. In essence, appreciation is one of the oldest tools we have for building community.

The evolutionary psychologist Robin Dunbar found that grooming was so central to early human bonding that language may have evolved as a more efficient form of "vocal grooming." Language helped us maintain larger social circles through conversation, storytelling, and expressions of gratitude. Just as a thank-you note or a heartfelt compliment strengthens bonds between people, grooming deepens relationships between primates. It signals "I see you. I value you. I want to stay connected." In both cases, appreciation is more than etiquette. It's a fundamental glue of social life and a quiet lever for unlocking future cooperation and opportunity.[9]

- *Who did something helpful for you recently?*
- *How could you demonstrate your appreciation?*
- *What appreciation practices will you bake into your life?*

8

Give Away Luck

*Luck favors the generous—goodwill sows
the seeds of serendipity.*

N ir Eyal has a simple but powerful philosophy of helping anyone who seeks his guidance. After writing *Hooked* and *Indistractable*, he made an open offer: Anyone interested can book a fifteen-minute conversation with him.[1] Over the past thirteen years, he has spoken with more than a thousand people, covering topics ranging from building healthy habits using the principles of *Hooked* to mastering focus and productivity from *Indistractable*. These complimentary discussions are not only an act of generosity but also a source of unexpected opportunity. While Nir genuinely offers his time to help others, he too benefits in tangible ways. A conversation might lead to a compelling story for one of his articles, providing insights that help others. It could spark a consulting engagement, a speaking opportunity, or, on rare occasions, an investment prospect. Each call is approached with an open mind and a genuine desire to be helpful, proving that generosity, when given freely, has a way of coming full circle.

This attitude of generosity has been the cornerstone of Nir's life, leading to so many wins. When he was younger, Nir was selling solar panels, going house to house asking if the owner was interested. In a few cases they were, but in most cases they were not. When Nir drilled down, he learned that many of those who didn't want solar panels were in the market for a heat pump, and that some houses were just not suited for solar panels at all given their location.

Instead of walking away without helping them, Nir recommended a local vendor who was doing an excellent job installing heat pumps, which would also help them lower energy costs. The heat-pump vendor, whom Nir did not know personally, found out that Nir was recommending him. He was thrilled because this was business that he never would have gotten otherwise. In return, the vendor started recommending Nir to customers who wanted solar panels! This was a win-win situation.

I met Nir when he reached out to me about referencing some of my work on luck for an article he was writing about luck in sales. I agreed to share the material and, in return, asked if he would be willing to talk with me about how luck had shaped his life. He agreed, and that conversation led to the story I shared above. Our dance of mutual support will surely continue, helping each of us expand our opportunities and collective luck. I share this story because it highlights how these exchanges often happen quietly behind the scenes. It's these unseen asks and offers that unlock luck.

Helping others is also a hallmark of great leadership. True leadership isn't about power or authority. It's about empowering others, offering support, and creating space for other people to shine. When individuals thrive, the entire organization rises. John Hennessy, with whom I have the privilege of working at Knight-Hennessy Scholars, exemplifies this kind of leadership. Before his current role, John served as the president of Stanford University for sixteen years. Even before I worked with him directly, John's influence was evident in the culture of the university. Stanford had become a place where experimentation was encouraged and innovation was celebrated. That wasn't by accident. John actively broke down silos across disciplines and created hubs that fostered cross-campus collaboration. His leadership was rooted in the belief that progress happens when people can pursue bold ideas together.

In a conversation on our six-part *Leading Matters* podcast,[2] John shared that his goal was always to help others realize their dreams and find success. Even in his own research, he consistently put his name last on publications, ensuring that students and junior faculty had the spotlight. That quiet generosity became a powerful force for the individuals he supported and the institution as a whole. Under his leadership, Stanford's reputation and rankings soared, and he continues to be recognized as a model of what leadership looks like when it's grounded in service.

You can begin cultivating luck at any point in your personal or professional life by offering, not asking for, five-minute favors. These simple yet meaningful acts create goodwill and open doors for others. These can be as effortless as recognizing a milestone or sharing an article that might be of interest. Providing a glowing introduction, either in person or in writing, is one of the most meaningful acts of generosity. Instead of having to toot their own horn, when you introduce someone by sharing the things you admire about them, be it their creativity or work ethic, you grease the wheels for them, providing valuable credibility.

These gestures also set the stage for reciprocity, a principle explored by Robert Cialdini in *Influence: The Psychology of Persuasion*.[3] His research demonstrates that when you help others, they feel an innate motivation to return the favor. Over time, your small acts of generosity strengthen relationships and increase the likelihood that you will catch the winds of luck in the form of favors that are returned to you in the future. In addition, when you are generous to one person, they are more likely to be generous to someone else. This is known as the "pay it forward" effect, described by the psychology professors Monica Y. Bartlett and David DeSteno,[4] as well as Adam Grant, who discusses it in *Give and Take*.[5] Givers, he writes, help others without the expectation of reciprocation. However, those who help others are much more likely to achieve long-term success by building a trusting community, leading to unexpected positive outcomes for everyone. What luck!

Grace Isford is a case in point. She started making small acts of generosity early in her career, tending her relationships like a garden. As an investor in frontier technology at Lux Capital and a resident of New York City, Grace was often asked whether a thriving AI ecosystem existed in the city. Rather than offering vague or anecdotal answers, she decided to dig deeper. She gathered everything she knew, conducted additional research, and compiled a thorough, data-driven response. At first she simply shared this knowledge with those who asked, but the findings proved so valuable that she took it a step further by publishing an article on Lux Capital's website. It was packed with resources for job seekers, investors, and entrepreneurs interested in New York's AI scene.

The response was overwhelming. Her article became a guide widely circulated among AI professionals. Soon, conference organizers and news outlets were inviting Grace to speak, cementing her reputation as an authority on AI in New York. As her visibility grew, so did her luck, including promising investment opportunities that began flowing her way. This all happened because she had freely shared her expertise.

But Grace didn't stop there. She continued to update the article with fresh news, ensuring it remained the go-to resource on the topic. Recognizing the power of the community, she expanded her impact even further by organizing an AI summit in New York, bringing together investors and entrepreneurs shaping the future of the industry. By helping others navigate the evolving AI landscape, Grace not only strengthened the broader technology community but also set in motion a ripple effect of opportunity in her own career. Her story is a salient reminder that generosity, including sharing knowledge to help others, can lead to a windfall of good luck all the way around.

You can intentionally weave generosity into the fabric of your work, making it the defining feature of your mission. Whether nonprofit or for-profit, nearly all successful ventures share a common thread: They solve someone else's problem. At the heart, these endeavors are acts of service, identifying pain points, unmet needs, or aspirations, and delivering scalable solutions.

Some ventures grow directly out of solving a personal problem that proves to be a challenge for others, too. Aya Mouallem, a PhD student in electrical engineering, co-founded All Girls Code in Lebanon with her collaborator, Maya Moussa.[6] The idea was sparked when Aya found herself one of only two girls in a software engineering class, and Maya was discouraged from pursuing computer engineering altogether. They realized that many girls in Lebanon weren't exploring opportunities in science and technology. It was not for lack of interest or talent but because they hadn't been encouraged to try. In response, they launched All Girls Code to provide girls with hands-on experiences in science, technology, engineering, and math (STEM), inspiring them to pursue paths they might not have otherwise considered.

What started as a small initiative where they taught basic coding skills to girls in Lebanon has grown into a dynamic movement, now powered by more than fifty passionate volunteers who are helping the next generation of girls across the Middle East and North Africa develop their skills and confidence. Today they have engaged over twenty-five hundred girls across the region, prioritizing those from underserved communities. All Girls Code now offers ongoing mentorship and runs hackathons and boot camps that allow girls to apply their new skills to address real-world problems, such as building a database for first responders and mapping the environment after local wildfires. Those who participate are delighted to give back by volunteering to help the organization as it grows.

As a result of this effort, All Girls Code has received recognition and awards, resulting in more opportunities for Aya and Maya to scale their impact. This includes national and global press for their work, invitations to speak with policy makers, meetings with world leaders, and the ability to attend conferences around the world.

Luck is often a direct result of helping others. What goes around doesn't just come around; it comes back bigger. Every time you solve someone's problem, share a resource, or lend a hand, you expand your circle of goodwill. As a result, they may be more likely to think of you when new opportunities arise. In this way, generosity becomes a magnet for good luck, not because you expect something in return but because your actions ripple outward, quietly shaping the environment in your favor.

- *Who could you help today?*
- *What small favors will be valuable to someone else?*
- *What lucky breaks have you experienced because of your past generosity?*

9

Attract Luck

*Luck favors those who build trust, an
invisible force that draws opportunity closer.*

Azza Cohen landed her dream job, serving as the official videographer for Vice President Kamala Harris at the White House. What an unbelievable opportunity for a young documentary filmmaker. She is so lucky! But let's pull back the curtain and see how this once-in-a-lifetime role really came to be.

While in college, Azza took a single documentary filmmaking class. It was the only one her school offered, and she was hooked. Despite knowing that film was an uncertain career path, she went all in. After the course, Azza stayed in close touch with her professor, keeping her posted on her progress. When she graduated, Azza landed a junior-level role at a small film production company in New York City. Shortly after joining, the company and the job fell apart at the seams.

Azza kept grinding, trying to make her way in film, and decided to go to graduate school to bolster her skills. The first person she contacted to talk about this decision was her professor. They continued to stay in close touch while she completed her degree, with Azza sending her drafts of her short films for feedback along the way. As graduation came into view, Azza started looking for jobs again. It felt nearly impossible, and Azza became completely demoralized. She had sent inquiries to over a hundred potential employers, including media outlets and newspapers, and nobody even wrote back to her. She confided in her professor that she was desperate to find a job that used her filmmaking skills. She just needed one job—one opportunity to get started. This should sound familiar, as earlier stories in this book also highlight the need for just one door to open to start a flywheel of good luck.

Around the same time, her professor happened to speak with a friend who had a unique challenge: finding the right person to document Kamala Harris's role as vice president. Who immediately came to mind? Azza! Within weeks, Azza was interviewing for the position. Soon after, she landed the job. From the outside it looks like blind luck. But looking behind the curtain, this opportunity would never have happened if Azza had not stayed in touch with her professor and built a trusting relationship over the course of a decade. The opportunity in the White House materialized exactly ten years after Azza took her first documentary class. Essentially, luck favors those who build relationships, invest in trust, and show up even when no immediate opportunity is in sight. That's the secret sauce behind Azza's lucky break.

In the early 1970s, the sociologist Mark Granovetter famously demonstrated the value of social ties in finding opportunities, because having a large number of social ties increases the surface area of opportunities to which you are exposed.[1] However, it is unlikely that those with whom you have ties will share those opportunities if they don't trust that the introduction will reflect well on them. This is crucial, but not often acknowledged.

Building trusting relationships takes time. You can't create them overnight. They must be earned, piece by piece, through consistent actions, reliability, and shared experiences. This reality became very clear to me when I transitioned from a role I had held for twenty years at Stanford University School of Engineering to a new position at Stanford's Knight-Hennessy Scholars. For two decades I had cultivated deep relationships, built a reputation, and accumulated goodwill at the engineering school. I assumed that all that trust, and the credibility I had carefully built, would naturally carry over with me. It didn't.

I quickly realized that despite being at the same university, I was entering a completely different social network, one in which my past relationships and reputation held little weight. The people in this new environment had little to no prior experience working with me, and trust doesn't transfer by default. It had to be re-earned in this new context.

Building trust in my new role was complicated by the COVID-19 lockdown. With everything remote, the organic, in-person moments of connection, such as spontaneous hallway conversations, were missing. Instead, every interaction was more formal and transactional. When I ran a workshop for the entire community of nearly two hundred students at our first in-person retreat, a student stood up to answer a question and continued standing after answering. I told the student that they "could sit down." My comment, innocently made, was interpreted as rude. Some students, whom I had never met in person before, were quick to interpret my casual comment as a criticism. Negative reactions continued over the coming weeks, and some students chose to spread doubt about my leadership of the organization. The situation was taking on a life of its own.

What should I do?

After much consideration, I decided to send a note to the entire community with the hope of turning things around. My letter said, "I am very sorry about my comment. If I could go back and do it again, I certainly would have handled the situation differently. . . . We are at the beginning of our story together. I hope we can write the next chapter where we move on and take the time to really get to know each other and to build trust. My door is always open, and I am eager to talk with anyone who wants to discuss this further."

The fact that I was willing to acknowledge the awkward situation and apologize for how my comment landed stopped the bleeding and allowed me to return to the task of building trust in the community. Several students who graduated that year sent me notes acknowledging that my letter was a turning point in their attitude toward me and an important leadership lesson for them.

Little by little, through consistent engagement, I could feel trust begin to build. Students were starting to assume the best rather than the worst and stopped questioning my intentions. I finally breathed a sigh of relief. It was a profound lesson: Trust isn't something you own but something you continuously earn.

I often think back to this transition when considering how trust functions in professional and personal networks. It's not enough to be competent or well-meaning. Others need to witness your behavior, experience your character, and come to believe through repeated interactions that you are someone on whom they can depend. Trust is fragile, and it can take years to build. But once it is established, it transforms everything from cautious interactions to confident collaboration.

In *What I Wish I Knew When I Was 20*, I shared my personal metaphor about building trust, which is worth repeating here:

> Every experience you have with someone else is a drop of water falling into a pool. As your experiences with that person grow, the drops accumulate, and the pool

deepens. Positive interactions are clear drops of water, and negative interactions are red drops of water. But they aren't equal. That is, a number of clear drops are needed to dilute one red drop, and that number differs for different people. Those who are very forgiving only need a few positive experiences—clear drops—to dilute a bad experience, while those who are less forgiving need a lot more to wash away the red. Also, the pool drains at different rates for different people. As a result, some people only pay attention to the experiences that have happened most recently, while others hold on to good and bad experiences for a very long time.

If you have a large reserve of positive experiences with someone, then one red drop is hardly noticed. It's like putting a drop of red ink into the ocean. But if you don't know a person well, one or two bad experiences stain the pool bright red. You can wash away negative interactions by flooding the pool with positive interactions until the red drops fade, but the deeper the red, the more work you have to do to cleanse the pool.

My letter to the community was my way of diluting the red drop that had fallen into our tiny pool of shared experiences. Over time, the pool has gotten much bigger, creating a much larger buffer of trust should another red drop fall, which in life is inevitable.

No matter how experienced, accomplished, or well-intentioned a person may be, trust must be built before meaningful progress can be made. Sarah Soule, who in 2025 was appointed dean of the Stanford Graduate School of Business, shared with me her journey of building trust within a new community. She quickly realized that even with a clear vision of what she wanted to accomplish, her ability to execute that vision depended on not just strategy but also trust. Without it, even the best-laid plans would falter.

For Sarah, building trust is not about persuading people to accept her ideas. Rather, it is about creating the conditions where people feel seen, valued, and included. That means listening deeply to those with vastly different perspectives, ensuring that they feel not just heard but truly understood, especially when they have significantly different points of view and desired outcomes.

This isn't about appeasement. Leadership requires making tough choices, and final decisions will inevitably alienate some people. Trust serves as the lubricant that allows forward momentum even when decisions don't fully align with everyone's desires. It reassures people that their voices will matter, the process will be fair, and leadership will be undertaken with integrity and not by someone's personal agenda. What Sarah experienced is what so many leaders encounter: Trust isn't just nice to have; it's the invisible force that determines whether ideas take flight or stall before they ever leave the ground. As the respected leadership authority Stephen Covey wrote, "Change happens at the speed of trust."[2]

One useful way to build trust is to actively learn what drives each person on your team. We each have a different relationship with our work, different ways we like to engage with others, and a long list of sometimes surprising preferences. One of my favorite ways to do this at work is to ask everyone on a team to write a personal user manual and to share it so that team members don't have to decode it by trial and error.

Some leaders publish their personal user manual, or a document on "how to work with me," to their entire company so they can be transparent about what they are like, and what they want and expect from others. Seasoned executive Ivar Kroghrud explained his reasons for sharing his user manual with his team in a *New York Times* interview.[3] He said that "if you lead people for a while, you realize that it's striking how different people are. If you use the exact same approach with two different people, you can get very different outcomes." Instead of turning it into a guessing game, with lots of potential mistakes, he decided to come right out and tell his team who he is and what he wants from others.

This exercise is most effective when executed by everyone on a team. I've learned that some people want direct feedback, others prefer to have it wrapped in positive comments; and there is an extremely wide variety of things that drive each of us crazy! Most importantly, the exercise opens the door for conversations about how the team will work together.

I've done this exercise with my team many times, and it always reveals surprising insights and helpful suggestions for how we work together, and ultimately builds trust within the team. Below are the ten questions I currently include in our personal user manual. You can craft others that fit your needs:

- What five words would you use to describe yourself?
- What qualities do you particularly value in others?
- What might others misunderstand about you?
- How can others earn a gold star from you?
- What behaviors drive you crazy, and why?
- What's the best way to convince you of something?
- How do you like to give feedback?
- How do you like to get feedback?
- What do you want to be recognized for?
- What is the best way to recognize you?

The third question is my favorite: "What might others misunderstand about you?" It always leads to interesting insights. For instance, an outgoing colleague admitted that they are actually quite shy. Knowing that, I am much better equipped to understand actions that were confusing in the past.

In sharing this idea with my students, one suggested that you could use this approach in dating, too, by crafting a set of questions specifically designed to help each person understand the other better. This brought to mind the famous thirty-six questions to fall in love.[4] Inspired by both the personal user manual and "thirty-six questions" exercises, I created the following set of questions for teams in my classes called "5 Questions to Fall in Love with Your Team," with the goal of helping them get to know each other quickly before they dive into their group project.

- What are your top priorities right now?
- What is your biggest challenge this week?
- How do you make an important decision?
- What times of day are you at your best?
- What is your favorite quote, and why?

Besides understanding each person, it's essential to know on whom you can truly rely for support. The world is filled with individuals who prioritize their own interests, but it's also home to those rare and dependable people who will stand by you when it matters most. Identifying these trusted allies can make all the difference, whether you're facing challenges, pursuing ambitious goals, or simply navigating the complexities of life. Surround yourself with those who uplift and encourage you because strong connections are the foundation of meaningful success.

In *Hope for Cynics: The Surprising Science of Human Goodness*, Jamil Zaki, a professor in the psychology department at Stanford, explores the intricate relationship between trust and cynicism.[5] He emphasizes that trust is the foundation of meaningful relationships and offers practical strategies for cultivating it. One of Jamil's key recommendations is to engage in deep, meaningful conversations that break down barriers. Surface-level interactions rarely foster genuine trust, but open, thoughtful dialogue helps people see each other as multidimensional and relatable, creating stronger, more authentic connections.

Jamil also underscores the power of vulnerability in building trust. When we openly share our struggles and weaknesses, we foster psychological safety, encouraging others to do the same. This mutual exchange of honesty strengthens relationships far more than maintaining a facade of perfection. Vulnerability is about creating space for authenticity and connection.

Beyond vulnerability, Jamil highlights the value of collaborating on shared projects as a useful trust-building tool. When people work together toward a common goal, they naturally develop a sense of mutual respect, accountability, and camaraderie. Collective success fosters trust more effectively than words alone, demonstrating reliability, competence, and shared purpose in real time. Taken together, these insights reinforce a core truth: Trust is cultivated through consistent, meaningful interactions, shared experiences, and the courage to be real with one another.

Trust isn't just important at work. It is equally important in your personal life. There are times, however, when it isn't clear what those in our life really need to foster trust. When my friend Sylvine called to tell me that she had breast cancer, I was deeply concerned. Two weeks later, she called me again and asked, "What happened?" I was confused. She continued, "I told you I was sick, and I haven't heard from you."

Baffled, I asked her what she wanted me to do. Her response was immediate and clear: "Call me every day." At first that sounded crazy. Wouldn't I be bothering her? But without hesitation, I agreed. And that request changed my life. Looking back, I realize that what she was really asking for was trust: trust that she wasn't alone in this; trust that she didn't have to reach out every time she needed support; trust that I would show up, consistently, without her having to ask.

Talking with Sylvine every day for eight years, sometimes for just a few minutes to check in and sometimes for hours, completely changed our relationship. We went from being good friends to being truly trusted friends. The texture of our relationship changed dramatically. Like a knitted scarf, the weave grew tighter and tighter, the bonds stronger and stronger as we continued to build trust.

There are many factors that conspire to interrupt building deep, trusting relationships. It is easy to rationalize that we don't have time to maintain relationships. However, developing and maintaining deep connections is one of the most important factors in living a meaningful and more healthful life. Many studies show that people with close relationships live longer than those who don't. Close friendships result in stronger immune systems, lower stress levels, improved self-confidence, and increased happiness. Trusted relationships are considered a "social vaccine" that inoculates us, improving our physical and mental health. Studies have shown that having close relationships is even more important than exercise in improving our general health. Therefore, trusting relationships don't just enrich our lives; they also quietly create good luck by making our lives better all the way around.

When Sylvine died, I realized that she had given me one of the biggest gifts I had ever received. She taught me what it means to really build trust by being fully engaged and responsive to those in our lives, even when it isn't easy. Having a foundation of trust invites good luck, because trusted friends and colleagues are more willing to share opportunities, make introductions, or extend a helping hand when they feel safe and seen. Trust creates a kind of relational gravity, drawing in the right chances that might otherwise pass by unnoticed.

- *What is on your personal user manual?*
- *What is on the personal user manual of others in your life?*
- *What will you do to build trust with those you care about?*

10

Unshackle Luck

*Luck favors those who untangle the knots
that tether opportunities.*

When I saw Michelle's message my jaw dropped, my heart started racing, and I have no idea what happened to my blood pressure. At first I was delighted to see my former student's name pop up in my inbox. I had known Michelle for years, through her undergraduate and graduate education. She had taken several of my courses and knew my work extremely well. In her message she shared that she was reading a book with a story that looked surprisingly like one in one of my books. The story was written in the first person, as though the author had lived my experiences. After a short back-and-forth, Michelle sent me screenshots of the pages.

My gut reaction was fury, and I considered all the ways I could react. Then I took a deep breath . . . I realized that I needed time to carefully consider the situation, since I knew that whatever decision I made would have consequences.

Still ruminating on my choices, I took a walk with my friend Loren. As we strolled along the coastal trail in Half Moon Bay, I shared my dilemma. She slowly turned to me and asked directly, "Who do you want to be in the world?"

The question stopped me in my tracks and reminded me to revisit my core values, as discussed in chapter 1. My uncertainty slowly melted away and I saw the situation with clearer eyes. Shifting my mode of thinking, I wondered if there could be a reasonable explanation for what happened.

I crafted an email to the author asking, "Can you help me understand what happened?" Within the hour I received a response asking to have a call the next day. During the call it became clear that the inclusion of my material was a sloppy mistake that should have been caught and corrected before publication. The author was humble and took full responsibility. Instead of making excuses, they offered to rectify the situation through a comprehensive set of actions that could be carried out immediately. I accepted the author's apology and their proposed solutions.

This could have blown up into a time-consuming conflict that would produce a tremendous amount of stress for us both. And to what end? It was better to rectify it and move on. The author and I stayed in touch and found that we had many mutual interests and colleagues in common. Four years later, I received a message from them, thanking me once again for giving them the benefit of the doubt when I didn't have to. The feeling I had when I received that message was incomparable. I knew I had made the right choice.

Resolving conflicts with intention and integrity reduces emotional friction. When conflicts remain unresolved, they drain our energy and create invisible barriers to new opportunities. Letting go of resentment and replacing it with understanding makes room for the kinds of encounters and partnerships that define good luck. Conflict resolution doesn't just lighten our emotional load; it actively increases the likelihood of luck finding us because we aren't distracted by the disagreement.

Research shows that conflict and stress lead to rumination, the act of mentally reliving experiences. Rumination reduces energy levels and resilience by decreasing motivation, increasing stress-inducing cortisol levels in the blood, and suppressing immune responses. Worrying about a conflict can literally make you sick.[1] As a result, it is much less likely that you will be able to focus on the things you really want to accomplish. The longer a conflict festers, the harder it is to tame. If prolonged, the stress can induce high blood pressure, ulcers, a weaker immune system, and depression.[2] Stress due to conflict can become an all-consuming distraction, pulling energy and attention away from the activities that matter to you. The conversations in your head are hijacked by the conflict, leaving little room for clarity, creativity, or the motivation needed to pursue your goals. Releasing the grip of conflict makes space for a clearer path toward what you want to achieve. This shift in mental energy improves your overall well-being and chances of encountering lucky breaks.

Martin (Marty) and Dorothie Hellman, who have been married for nearly sixty years, unlocked the secret to a conflict-free marriage. Marty is a cryptographer, known for his groundbreaking work that protects the security of internet transactions. Earlier in their marriage, Dorothie and Marty found themselves bickering daily. As a peace activist, Dorothie challenged Marty, a passionate supporter of nuclear disarmament, to find a way to solve the conflicts in their own marriage. She told him that if they didn't do this, their marriage was over. Marty was therefore highly motivated to figure it out. As gifted problem-solvers, he and Dorothie took on the challenge of reducing friction in their marriage.

With this task in front of them, together Marty and Dorothie spent months unpacking why they were fighting and how to resolve their conflicts. They realized that they first needed to let go of their own egos, defensiveness, and inclination to blame each other. They also needed to focus on deeply understanding the other person by carefully listening to their perspective. And they recognized that they needed to rebuild trust, because its absence led to fearful, destructive behavior that would often spiral out of control.

They captured what they learned in a book on conflict resolution titled *A New Map for Relationships*.[3] The book title derives from the first story in the book, about a day trip Marty and Dorothie took to an event in San Francisco many years ago. When they had to figure out how to navigate to their next destination, they pulled over and Dorothie took out a large paper map, since GPS was not yet available. Marty reached over and grabbed the map out of Dorothie's hands. She was furious! After ripping up the map, Dorothie stormed out of the car, slamming the door behind her. Marty sat there, not knowing what to do next.

When Dorothie calmed down enough to get back in the parked car, there were several moments of high tension that were broken when they both started laughing. They had spent enough time analyzing how to diffuse their conflicts to reduce the tension. More laughter followed when they had to put together the pieces of the map, which were scattered all over the car, to find their way to the event.

Dorothie and Marty used the tools they had developed to resolve their conflict. Most important, they learned to ask each other questions instead of just getting mad, which they call "get curious, not furious." Over time, their conflict-resolution skills improved to the point that they no longer argued to resolve issues, and they both attest that they haven't had a fight in twenty years! Marty and Dorothie learned that "differences of opinion, which used to become fights over who was right, could be transformed into opportunities to expand their perspectives and learn from one another."[4] They use these tools every day to repair and strengthen their relationship. If they had not, their marriage would not have survived.

What Marty and Dorothie discovered is something we

can all learn: Conflict doesn't have to be destructive. When approached with curiosity and care, conflict can become a catalyst for growth and connection. But doing so takes more than good intentions. It requires practiced skills that fortunately can be taught and developed.

This process begins with open and thoughtful dialogue to foster mutual understanding, where you share your perspective and make a genuine effort to understand the other person's point of view. At KHS, Thay Graciano, a PhD student studying political communication and deliberative democracy, and I developed a workshop for the KHS community to facilitate navigating difficult conversations. This is a particularly important skill in our highly diverse community of students, who have very different life experiences and perspectives.

Thay grew up in southern Brazil with great scarcity and greater corruption. When she was fourteen, Thay and her family moved to London to escape poverty, and she worked cleaning houses to survive. She met a young man who saw her promise and potential, and helped her tell a different story about her future. With his encouragement, she applied to college, where she received a scholarship. Thay is now studying conflict resolution on a global scale with the goal of finding ways for those with very different ideologies to talk with one another to unravel the knot of poverty and to tell more empowering stories about what is possible in their lives.

The framework that Thay and I developed categorizes discussions into personal or professional topics, and those centered on either behaviors or values. By offering this structured approach, our goal is to enable others to engage more effectively with those who hold vastly different perspectives, fostering a culture of respectful dialogue and problem-solving.

The resulting 2 x 2 matrix on the following page shows how this works, with an example conflict in each quadrant:

- Some conflicts relate to an individual's behavior, such as leaving socks on the floor.
- Some conflicts relate to professional behavior, such as interrupting in meetings.
- Some conflicts relate to personal values, such as monogamy in marriage.
- Some conflicts relate to professional values, such as diversity initiatives at work.

The conflicts in each quadrant arise from the clash of perspectives, and each requires a different type of conversation to diffuse, rather than escalate, the conflict. Understanding what type of conversation you are having before engaging is crucial to avoid a conflagration. In class we emphasize the importance of focusing on the impact the specific behavior has on you by using "I statements." For example, "When you leave your socks on the floor, I feel frustrated that our house isn't tidy" as opposed to "When you leave your socks on the floor, you are disrespectful." This avoids assigning intention

Personal

Monogamy	Picking up socks
Diversity Initiatives	Interrupting in meetings

Values   Behavior

Professional

or "crossing the net" into assuming that you know what the other person is thinking or feeling, which could add fuel to the conflict. This type of communication was pioneered by Marshall Rosenberg, who launched and led the Center for Nonviolent Communication.

Values-based conflicts require a different type of conversation in which you lead with curiosity and avoid accusations and assumptions. Those conversations should begin with inquiries such as "Tell me why you believe that" or "Help me understand your point of view." You may never agree on whether monogamy or diversity efforts are appropriate, but you will gain an understanding of the other person's perspective and learn something new in the process.

There is an art and science to these types of discussions

because disagreements about behaviors are usually rooted in differences in values. So, you might need to move back and forth—from right to left—focusing on behaviors and how they are influenced by values, and back again. For example, if you are discussing a conflict about a behavior, such as how to load the dishwasher or where to spend the holidays, you might need to unpack why this is an important issue for the other person instead of focusing only on the specific behavior.

One of my favorite books is Alain de Botton's *The Course of Love*, which traces a relationship between a couple, Rabih and Kirsten, from the first seeds of their courtship through their marriage.[5] Whenever there is a conflict, he shows us what it looks like on the ground, and then he pops up to explain what it is "really about." The eye-opening explanations about tensions that arise when buying glassware at IKEA, or whether to keep the window in their bedroom open or closed, help us see the conflicting values behind each of the disagreements. Now whenever I get into a conflict, I am primed to consider what it is *really about*, not what it appears to be about, starting with the behavior and then shifting to value differences when needed.

In addition to directly resolving conflicts, we can also learn to be more forgiving. Fred Luskin spent decades studying forgiveness, and he captures his insights in his books, including *Forgive for Good: A Proven Prescription for Health and Happiness*.[6] He posits that forgiveness is a choice, and holding a grudge harms the victim more than the offender.

Forgiving someone, no matter how terrible the transgression, builds self-confidence and optimism, and reduces depression and stress. Luskin makes clear that forgiveness doesn't mean condoning or forgetting transgressions but is instead a gift that you give yourself. That is a bold idea: Forgiveness is for you, not the other person. Forgiveness frees you to focus on more important objectives in your life. In the context of luck, that matters. It's hard to hoist a sail when your hands are tied. Letting go of resentment frees you to focus on what truly matters to you.

Having tools to resolve and release conflicts is extraordinarily empowering. Consider the story of a former White House advisor who, for reasons that will become clear, asked me not to share his name.

Tensions frequently run hot in the high-stakes world of Washington politics, where people with conflicting views are thrust together in the policy-making process. Public officials often disagree with each other as they work through the policies that they are handling together. More than a decade ago, this advisor, on leave from his university, recommended that the president reject a proposal made by a senior agency official. The official, furious at being criticized, retaliated by pushing to have the advisor removed. The attempt failed, but the damage was done. From that point on, the interactions between the advisor and agency official were overshadowed with tension, each meeting thick with unspoken resentment.

Fast-forward a few years. The advisor had returned to

his academic post, and the agency official was now being considered for a leadership role at another university. Low and behold, the advisor received from that university an unexpected request for a confidential letter of support for the former agency official. The advisor now had a choice: Should he set aside the grudge against the person who tried to ruin him?

After reflecting, the advisor chose to forgive. He wrote a strong letter of support, recognizing that their past conflict had been fueled by the pressures of their environment. Releasing the grudge was liberating, and the fact that his former rival had no idea he had written the glowing letter was even more freeing.

As the years passed, the two former rivals had occasional contact. The fact that the former advisor had quietly forgiven the official created more openness and set the stage to move past their conflict. Eventually the former agency official expressed both an appreciation for the past work of the former adviser and a desire to collaborate given their common interests. This led to new opportunities to work together, including celebrating the accomplishments of a shared mentor. Releasing resentment isn't just an act of grace. It's an investment in future good luck.

Finally, no matter how keen your judgment, you never know what is going on in someone else's life. Often people who treat you badly have something going on in their life that is tearing them apart. Everyone is carrying around a lifetime of wounds, some of which are very fresh. By giving grace, you can support others and help yourself by harboring no negative feelings.

Several years ago, a student was late for my class. There were clear rules about being on time, with consequences for repeated tardiness. When he entered an hour into the two-hour class, I could have chastised him for missing the bulk of the session. But I took a deep breath before approaching him and asked, "What is going on? Are you okay?" He told me that his family was in Syria, and his grandmother's house had been bombed that morning. What a shock! Imagine how I would have felt if I had criticized him for being late. Even when there are rules, there needs to be room for understanding. If you start with curiosity, you can avoid conflicts that hurt others and weigh you down. Treat everyone as if they have a broken heart, because they probably do. Luck favors those who forgive.

- *What conflicts are consuming your attention right now?*
- *How are those conflicts a direct response to specific behaviors or value differences?*
- *How can you resolve those conflicts to free your mind to capture more positive opportunities?*

Part 3
Hoist Your Sail

The harder I work, the luckier I get.

—*Unknown*

11

Leap Toward Luck

*Luck favors those who take risks, each one
a stepping stone toward success.*

Rumi wrote, "The path appears only when you begin to
walk."

What a powerful concept: you won't know where the
road will take you until you begin the journey. After your
first step, the path begins to unfold. Nothing will happen until you take the first step. If you want to run a race, this is obvious. But it is also true with any other endeavor. If you want
to learn to play the piano, you need to first sit down at the
keyboard. If you want a job, you need to apply. If you want
to be a stand-up comedian, you need to get on stage! There
is a big difference between saying you want to do something
and actually doing it.

Case in point: Four years ago, my neighbor Monique was
ready to find a life partner and determined to put herself out
there to meet someone special. But after long workweeks,

the last thing she wanted to do was go out. Instead, she'd slip into her pajamas, curl up in bed with a good book, and drift off to sleep. Clearly she wasn't going to meet anyone that way.

One Friday evening, a friend showed up at her door and insisted that they go to a party, refusing to take no for an answer. Monique protested. She was already in bed. But her friend was relentless. She had to go out! Finally, with great reluctance, Monique threw on a jacket over her pajamas, pulled on her boots, and walked out the door. With no makeup and unbrushed hair, she made a concession to her persistent friend.

They ended up at a bar on the south side of San Francisco, the kind of place Monique would never have gone alone. Sitting in the corner, wishing she were home, she was surprised when someone sent her a drink. Sipping it slowly, she began to relax. The pounding music coaxed her from her seat, and she joined her friend on the dance floor. That's when she saw him. As if in a movie, Monique's eyes locked onto a man across the room. His face was mostly hidden behind a COVID face mask, but that didn't matter. There was something about him. They started dancing.

As it turned out, Peter had also come to the party reluctantly. After a long week, he had nearly stayed home, too, but his friends had convinced him otherwise. At the end of the night, Peter helped Monique get a taxi and went home, wondering how long he should wait before calling her to make another date. She beat him to it. At 8:30 the next morning, Monique phoned Peter.

The rest, as they say, is history. They didn't part for two weeks, one of which Monique spent sick with COVID, and the other included a spontaneous weekend getaway in Napa. On the way home from Napa, Peter took a detour . . . to buy an engagement ring! Monique had been ready to find her person, but it never would have happened if she hadn't taken that first step and put on her jacket (even over her pajamas!) and walked out the door. Four years later, they are still married and exceedingly happy that they both took a leap that night.

That first step is sometimes the hardest. Sometimes it isn't a choice. You can get pulled (like Monique), you can get pushed, and there are times when you actively jump!

Getting pulled happens when an attractive opportunity falls into your lap. You bid farewell to your old life as you get pulled into a new one. It would be great if you could will these opportunities into existence, but they are rare. You can't plan on a "prince or princess" showing up to pull you into a new life, but it can happen!

Many years ago, Alberto Savoia got a call from a friend whose car had broken down. The friend had a job interview that day and had no way to get there. Though it meant dropping everything at work, Alberto reluctantly agreed to give him a ride. While waiting in the reception area as his friend interviewed, a man approached and asked if he needed help. "No," Alberto replied, "I'm just waiting for my friend." The man struck up a conversation and asked if Alberto knew how to code. "Yes," he said, he did. The conversation continued, and the man encouraged Alberto to apply for a job at the company, a little-known start-up called Sun Microsystems. Alberto wasn't looking for a new job; he was happy where he was. But he took a chance by throwing his hat into the ring. A week later, he received a job offer at the new company. He was essentially pulled into that new role, which unlocked a wave of good luck as the company grew. That encounter launched a thirteen-year career at Sun Microsystems, which grew into a $200 billion business. The man who approached him? It was Eric Schmidt, then vice president of engineering.

Fast-forward a couple of decades, and Eric Schmidt was now CEO of another small start-up called Google. Eric Schmidt reconnected with Alberto and offered him another role. Once again, Alberto was pulled into this new opportunity, becoming the company's first engineering director, leading to the next wave of good luck. Neither opportunity was planned or even sought after—Alberto was pulled.

The opposite of getting pulled is getting pushed. It could be getting fired from your job, getting dumped by your partner, or learning you are pregnant. These discontinuities in your life compel you to change course. They force you to question everything, to do things you wouldn't have considered before, and to make real changes.

For example, Janine Zacharia can't remember a time when she didn't want to be a reporter. From the time she was a child, she loved the news and had an insatiable desire to understand how the world works. Curious to the bone, she observes closely, asks lots of questions, and loves telling stories about what she sees. Even at nine years old, she was narrating her family's trip at Disneyland, pretending that she was a roving reporter. Her dream came true after years of preparation when, in her thirties, Janine became the Jerusalem bureau chief for *The Washington Post*. The job was exhilarating, playing to all her strengths, and energized her every day as she gathered information and sent in stories from the front lines as history was being made.

In January 2011, however, Janine needed to make a difficult decision. Three months pregnant with her first child, she was reporting on the Arab Spring in Cairo. Looking out of her hotel window, she could see growing conflict as protestors and security forces engaged fiercely. Tear gas was in the air, and Janine knew that it was unsafe to go outside, both for herself and her unborn child. She found herself searching online for the effects of tear gas on pregnant mothers. She knew she was getting pushed out of the job she loved because of her new responsibilities.

Even though Janine loved her job, one that she had worked so hard to achieve, she needed to start over and focus on her growing family. So, she quit, moved to California to be with her husband, and reinvented her life as a faculty member at Stanford. Janine started at the bottom of the ladder after living on the top rung, including flying around the world with the US secretary of state. With determination and grit, Janine built her reputation all over again, shedding one persona for another, until she regained the respect and credibility she had before but in a completely different setting.

Sometimes you don't get pulled or pushed—you jump! This happens when you stretch your risk profile, as discussed in chapter 3, leaving a situation that is fine, even good, in the quest for something better. Jumping requires a lot of activation energy because it is hard to leave something that is good enough, especially when the alternative is undefined. There are lots of times when people want to jump; they dream of jumping and know there is something better on the other side, but they can't muster the energy to do it. But look what can happen when you do!

Consider the story of Sarahi Espinoza Salamanca, born in Mexico and a recent Knight-Hennessy scholar. Knowing her background, you might be surprised that she was a graduate student at Stanford. She made it happen by taking leap after leap after leap.

Sarahi was undocumented, living in North Hollywood when she was in high school, the youngest of eleven children. She did well in school and expected to go to the University of California, Los Angeles. However, when she talked to the guidance counselor, she was told, "People like you don't go to college." Sarahi was shocked. She knew she was from an immigrant family but didn't know what it meant to be undocumented. She felt so alone, without any knowledge of others in her position. She soon learned that she couldn't get a job or go to school without having a US Social Security number. So, she moved back to her hometown of East Palo Alto, California, to live with her sister. She worked as a babysitter, earning enough to live a simple life, which she expected to continue indefinitely. She got married and planned to start a family. She was happy.

Soon thereafter, as fortune would have it, President Barack Obama passed the Deferred Action for Childhood Arrivals (DACA) program, which allowed young people who were born outside the US to get a US Social Security number and go to school and to work. Sarahi was worried about the visibility but took a leap and applied. After she received her Social Security number, Sarahi enrolled in the local community college. That same year she saw a flier on a school bulletin board to work for the Girl Scouts. She took a chance by applying and was hired to teach in Bay Area elementary schools, and she started a dozen new Girl Scout troops.

While doing this, Sarahi stumbled upon an announcement for an Innovators Challenge by Voto Latino to use technology to solve a problem. Sarahi decided to take another leap! Without any background in developing software, she pushed ahead to build a searchable database to help undocumented students find scholarships. She pitched the idea and was selected as one of the top submissions in the country.

Sarahi arrived in Washington, DC, for the event and was overwhelmed. The other six teams were majority men, and each was accompanied by a team of supporters. And, hers was the only project from a community college. Sarahi called her mother, sharing her anxiety. Her mother pumped her up, saying, "Just tell your story. Close your eyes, say a prayer, and just be you." She got up to give her pitch with faith and confidence, and won first place, awarding her $100,000 to build a mobile app named DREAMers Roadmap.

Without any experience building a nonprofit venture, Sarahi asked everyone she knew for help, an approach discussed in chapter 6. Since then, thirty-four thousand students have used the application, and Sarahi is responsible for helping them access millions of dollars in funding for college. Seven years later, at thirty-two years old, Sarahi took another chance and applied to Santa Clara University, where she finally graduated from college. Before her graduation, she took another chance and applied to Stanford for graduate school. She was thirty-four years old when she began, more than a decade older than most of her classmates. Sarahi credits her mother for her faith, fearless attitude, and her willingness to take leaps into the unknown. Her mother always told Sarahi that there is never a bad outcome. You either win or learn.

Luck erupts in your life when you take a chance. Sometimes you get pulled, sometimes you get pushed, and sometimes you need to jump!

- *When in your life have you been pulled, pushed, or jumped?*
- *How might you invite luck into your life by taking a chance?*
- *Is there somewhere you would like to jump?*

12

Invite Luck

Luck favors those who stir the pot,
creating room for surprises.

After watching my TED Talk on luck, Oliver Green-wald, a recent college graduate, reached out to me. He shared that the talk captured so many things he already does to make himself lucky. He also recognized that most people don't use the approaches I described to unlock their own luck. That realization sparked an idea: He would become a "luck coach," helping others amplify their own good fortune. He wanted to get my thoughts on the idea. My immediate reaction? Fabulous! So many could benefit from having a personal luck coach.

After our call, it was clear that Oliver is a luck magnet. His secret sauce? Injecting randomness into his life almost daily and then building on those opportunities. He put this approach to the test right after college by moving to Japan for a year, despite having no job, no contacts, and no safety net. To create his own luck, he made a conscious effort to meet new people, to say yes to everything, and to always follow up on every opportunity, invitation, and introduction.

To get started, Oliver made it a habit to visit the local coffee shop every day. One afternoon, he struck up a conversation with a group of young people enjoying their coffee. They hit it off, and Oliver would have loved to continue their conversation. However, there was no clear reason they'd even see each other again. So, thinking on his feet, Oliver told them he was hosting a barbecue later that week—an event he invented on the spot—and invited them to join. They accepted, and over time they became close friends.

In another instance, a new friend advised Oliver that the best way to kick-start his time in Tokyo was to go to the Breakfast Club and ask for Luli. Without hesitation, Oliver followed the advice. He arrived at the diner and asked for Luli, who, as it turned out, was the manager. She welcomed him with open arms and, even though the diner was closed at the time, invited him to stick around. While there, he struck up a conversation with one of the staff members, who then introduced him to the owner of a local company. That connection led to a job offer.

Oliver was thrilled. He had applied to dozens upon dozens of jobs without success. All he needed was one offer! This job turned out to be the perfect fit, far better than he had imagined. Among his responsibilities was organizing a conference in the Kingdom of Bhutan. Another was to design a digital scavenger hunt to celebrate the New Year. And to think, it all happened because he walked into the Breakfast Club and introduced himself. After hearing this story, I looked up an article about the Breakfast Club and found that its philosophy can be summed up as follows: "Let's eat together! Let's drink together! Let's talk and hang together! Let's draw and write together! Let's sing, play, and dance together! Come on and join us!" This approach certainly worked for Oliver.

Oliver has experimented with lots of ways of injecting randomness into his life with the hope of catching luck. One of my favorites is always carrying a big umbrella. When it rains, he looks for people who don't have one, and he walks up beside them and offers to walk with them to their destination. Sometimes people think he is strange and rebuff him, but in many cases he has met some interesting people who are appreciative of his kind offer. One interaction even led to a date with a girl who was delighted to stay dry in the rain.

Oliver plants lots of seeds for luck to sprout over time as he moves through the world. A simple but powerful example is celebrating others, as discussed in more depth in chapter 7. As a designer, when he used a web-based application that he thought worked well, he took the time to write a note to the company thanking them for their great user interface. The company founder was tickled to get Oliver's positive comments and asked to talk with him to get more specific feedback about what he found most useful. Flash-forward several years, and Oliver was looking for a product design job. He reached out to the founder, who was happy to interview him for the role. How lucky for Oliver!

This is just a taste of how Oliver stirs a little randomness into his routine to cook up lucky opportunities. He knows that luck often strikes in unexpected ways. Therefore he makes a habit of trying all sorts of new things. When he spots a spark of possibility, he fans the flames and keeps the magic alive. It's this mix of curiosity, courage, and follow-through that makes him a stellar luck coach.

It turns out Oliver picked up many of his lucky super-powers from his mother, Rachel Greenwald, a professional matchmaker. Rachel taught him to keep an open mind when making connections. In love, she said, you've got to widen the aperture. Don't eliminate potential matches too soon or filter for traits that don't correlate with long-term happiness, such as hair color or height. She also had this rule: Never drink coffee alone at home. Go to a coffee shop and talk to people. She's even been known to toss out her clients' coffee pots to reinforce the message. It worked for Oliver!

Rachel also reminded Oliver that everyone brings something to the table. Some lead with good looks; others shine through humor, integrity, or a sense of adventure. And even if someone isn't a match for you, they might be perfect for someone else you know. Just imagine the goodwill you generate by introducing your date to your best friend, who might be a better match. Finally, Rachel urges her clients to take a long-term view when dating. Learning this, one of her clients, after realizing that her date wasn't the right fit for her, stayed curious and open. During their conversation, she asked him how he meets new people. Her date mentioned a lunch-dating club that he frequented. She looked it up when she got home, joined herself . . . and by her second lunch she'd met her match! That would not have happened if she hadn't been open to learning something new during the date.

Every decision you make, no matter how small, reshapes the trajectory of your life. Matt Haig illustrates this beautifully in *The Midnight Library*, a novel that explores how even the smallest choices can lead to vastly different futures. Haig writes, "Every life contains millions of decisions. Some big, some small. But every time one decision is taken over another, the outcome differs. An irreversible variation occurs, which in turn leads to further variations."[1] In the book, the protagonist finds herself in a magical library in which each book represents a different version of her life, each path branching from a single choice that altered her life course. I love that not only does her journey change but so does her physical appearance. By opening different doors and following those paths, we truly change who we become. We are each always one decision away from a completely different life!

This concept is consistent with the idea of the "adjacent possible," a term introduced by the theoretical biologist Stuart Kauffman in his 2000 book, *Investigations*.[2] This framework describes how an endless number of potential futures exist, each just waiting to be unlocked. Each choice you make doesn't just open new doors; it creates entirely new futures that didn't previously exist. A classic example is the evolution of the eye, which is stunningly complex. The eye could never have evolved until the first simple, light-sensitive cell emerged millions of years ago. Once the door to vision was opened with one single photoreceptor, the possibility for a more sophisticated visual system emerged. Oliver's story, *The Midnight Library*, and the adjacent possible framework remind us that every decision, no matter how small, has the potential to expand the canvas of possibilities ahead.

Those who are lucky exploit this concept and try lots of things, keeping what works by inviting individuals and ideas into their life. They relentlessly open metaphorical doors to peer at what is behind them. Opening doors includes meeting new people, listening to new music, and taking the long way home, and then building on those connections when you find something of interest. Not all doors lead to a gold mine, but you'll never know unless you try.

It is possible to be explicit about adding randomness into your life to see what materializes. For example, before I turned sixty, I gave myself an assignment that I called "60 Weeks to 60." The idea was that I would try something new every week before this milestone birthday. One week I took photos of things I had never noticed before in my neighborhood. Another week I made a new art piece each day using materials I found around the house. Some projects lasted more than a single week, such as the several (really useful) weeks I spent meeting with a public-speaking coach, and the month I spent trying to learn French (*pas suffit*!) Some projects were easy, such as writing daily thank-you notes; some were more challenging, such as going to bed much earlier.

I was delighted that some of these small experiments stuck and became a regular part of my life. My daily art project became a hobby after I started making collages from the covers of *The New Yorker* magazines I had stacked up on my bedside table. I began by picking out three covers, which I cut into strips and pasted together in an interesting pattern, as seen below. So tickled by the results, I continued experimenting with lots of variations using dozens of covers. Now the walls of my office have large prints of many of these collages, and I created greeting cards that I use for thank-you notes. This new hobby never would have materialized

if I hadn't given myself the assignment to inject randomness into my life.

Every day, we each engage in a dance with the world. Some things happen to us, such as unexpected invitations, coincidences, and setbacks beyond our control. Other times, we shake things up ourselves by adding something new. Adding randomness isn't about relinquishing control. It's about expanding possibility. It's not chaos for chaos's sake; it's deliberate disruption. When you step off your usual path, you increase the odds of encountering something or someone that shifts your trajectory. These new inputs lead to new possibilities, break patterns, spark ideas, and surface opportunities that routines never would have revealed.

- *What can you do to add randomness to your life?*
- *What experiments could you perform that could open the door to a new world of possibilities?*
- *How have chance encounters resulted in luck in your life already?*

13

Scaffold Luck

Luck favors those who build on small victories, creating ladders to larger wins.

f I have one luck superpower, it's this: I've learned how to build on tiny wins again and again and again. Even the smallest spark of possibility can grow into an inferno if you add fuel and fan it. Unfortunately, most people ignore those sparks or even stamp them out. However, if you notice them and feed them with focused effort, that spark becomes a flame, and the flame can grow into a mighty blaze. The key isn't waiting for a wildfire to appear; it's learning to recognize the tiny sparks and choosing to tend them. From the outside, your success may look like blind luck. But behind the scenes, you will know that it is the result of steady attention and repeated effort. Like small but consistent investments, modest actions compound over time, resulting in significant wins.

Below is my personal story, illustrating how I fueled small

sparks—tiny opportunities that grew into something much more significant. In some cases, the sparks go out despite my efforts. But in many cases, just a little bit more effort and attention lead to remarkable results. Notice when and where I lean into an opportunity that others might ignore, as well as places I could have built on the opportunity in front of me but didn't.

When my son Josh was sixteen—twenty years ago—I realized that in just a couple of years he'd be heading off to college. I feared that I hadn't taught him all that I wanted to about how to navigate the world. So, I began making a list. It started as a simple document on my computer with a list of thoughts, such as "See problems as opportunities" and "Challenge assumptions." I updated it periodically.

A few months after I started this list, I was asked to give a talk to a small group of undergraduate students who were just slightly older than Josh. I decided to use my list for inspiration and created a raw, impromptu slide deck, with the title "What I Wish I Knew When I Was 20." The talk went well, and I was invited to present it again to another group. Feeling encouraged, I began offering the lecture to other groups across campus. With each new lecture, I refined the presentation, adding more details, examples, and depth.

Later that year I planned to attend an entrepreneurship educators conference with several hundred participants. I proposed to deliver this same lecture, and to my delight, my proposal was accepted. At the conference, an attendee from the United States Military Academy, or West Point, attended my session and soon thereafter invited me to present the same lecture to all their first-year cadets. What luck! Of course, I accepted.

The response to the West Point lecture was very encouraging, and I began to think that maybe the content would work as a book. On my flight home I started drafting a book proposal. I was so engrossed in the process that when the flight attendant reached across me to hand a glass of water to the gentleman seated next to me, I was startled and accidentally bumped his hand, spilling the entire glass of water into my computer. When I got home, I dried out my laptop and finished the proposal.

I shared the book proposal with my colleague Bob Sutton, who has written many successful books. Bob suggested I send it to his book agent. The agent, after reading it, wrote back, "It's not soup yet," quoting an old Lipton soup commercial from the 1970s. I was disappointed and set aside the book proposal. At that time, I wasn't fully committed to the project and let that rejection stop me in my tracks.

A year later, on an early morning flight from San Francisco to Miami, I found myself sitting next to Mark Tauber, the publisher of an imprint of HarperCollins. After chatting for a couple of hours, I took the risk of sharing my book proposal with him, which was still on my laptop. Mark was kind enough to scan it, but he said, "No thank you. This isn't for us." Despite my disappointment, we continued our conversation and exchanged contact information at the end of the flight.

The story could easily have ended there, but I decided to take a tiny risk. Several months after our flight, I invited Mark to be a guest at my creativity course in which we were imagining the future of the publishing industry. (I had to select a topic for our class project. Why not this?) Mark agreed to join us, and it was a productive experience for all involved. The students shared their innovative ideas, and Mark shared his perspective as an industry insider.

A few months later, I reached out to Mark again, this time sharing a few short video presentations from my students' submissions to our Global Innovation Tournament. Intrigued, he mentioned that one project might have potential for a book. He was interested in publishing a book with my students, but not with me! That was another disappointment, but no matter. I coordinated a meeting with the students. He came to campus along with a senior editor, Gideon Weil. The students were graduating, and frankly not interested in writing a book together. Over lunch, Gideon turned to me and asked, "Have you considered writing a book?" I said, "Why yes, I have!" and gave him the exact same proposal that had been passed over by Mark on the plane a year earlier, and by the book agent another year before that. Within two weeks I had a book contract and agreed to write the book in just four months so that it could be ready in time for the following year's college graduations.

The writing process began immediately. Every day I buckled down to write from 6 a.m. to 9 a.m. before heading to work. I sought out people with interesting backgrounds for lunch or a phone call and mined the conversations for relevant stories. Every night before turning in, I reviewed my notes from that day's conversations, pulling out the gems, and the next morning I incorporated those stories into the book. I also included examples from my classes and related research. The book manuscript was delivered three years after I started Josh's list, and the book was released on Josh's twentieth birthday.

You might think, "Well, you were at Stanford University, so you started from an incredibly fortunate position." And you'd be right. I have been fortunate and lucky. However, my career at Stanford didn't materialize out of thin air. I used the same strategy to get a job at the university.

Let's go back in time . . .

As mentioned in chapter 4, in 1999 I took a junior position at Stanford because I was excited by the chance to join a dynamic team working on a fascinating project, launching the new entrepreneurship center in the School of Engineering. Over the next thirteen years I carved a path that ultimately led to my appointment as a Professor of the Practice. For many, I was a unicorn, since this leap was literally inconceivable.

Here's how I did it:

First, I made my intentions clear, asking for what I wanted

and sharing my goals with my close colleagues. With that North Star, I pursued every opportunity I could that would lead me closer to that goal. This involved stretching beyond my assigned role whenever possible. I also helped colleagues solve nagging problems, developed new programs that showcased my colleagues' work, and volunteered to take on tasks they didn't want. Little by little, my credibility grew.

The winds of luck picked up when Bob Sutton decided not to teach a course on creativity that he had previously taught for many years. Nobody else wanted to do it, so I jumped at the chance and volunteered to teach it. "Pick me! Pick me!" I said. Honestly, it was a stretch. But I put together a plan that was low-risk by inviting a wide range of experts to share their work with the class each week. After teaching the course for a few years, each time with an inspiring co-instructor, I slowly but surely became an expert, too, and could remove the guardrails of guest speakers. I started developing my own classroom exercises and inventing new frameworks describing the creative process. After teaching this topic for ten years—the time equivalent of completing a couple PhDs—I wrote and published two books on creativity and innovation. This credibility set the stage for my appointment as Professor of the Practice.

You might say, "But you already had a PhD from Stanford's School of Medicine, and that surely opened doors for you." Again, let's go back in time. . . . My graduate school opportunity came about only because I employed the same strategies described above. It began with me writing letters—actual paper letters with stamps—to every neuroscience faculty member at Stanford to inquire if they needed a research assistant. Everyone wrote back to me, saying no.

My résumé ended up getting passed around within the Department of Anesthesiology, and I was, surprisingly, offered a short-term job testing the newly invented oximeters in the operating room. I jumped at it! When that job ended, I literally knocked on doors throughout the entire medical school and ultimately convinced another faculty member to hire me as a research assistant. After a few months in that lab, I asked if I could do some of my own experiments. I was offered the opportunity to do so if I did my experiments after working hours. After a few months, my future advisor agreed to support me as a graduate student, and I applied to the PhD program. Acceptance was far from guaranteed, and I was told I would be considered contingent upon my jumping through what felt like flaming hoops to demonstrate my viability. Eventually I was admitted.

Am I lucky? Absolutely! But that luck didn't just fall into my lap. It materialized because of a long series of tiny risks, false starts, disappointments, and, most importantly, learning to build on every bit of momentum that came my way. I am not special at all. I'm just willing to keep trying lots of things. Each small success becomes a stepping stone for the next, so long as I just keep building on them.

I see so many people giving up on their dreams when they hit a roadblock, as I did when my book proposal was first rejected by the book agent. I now know from experience that good luck is the result of an ongoing commitment to a goal and the willingness to continue trying little experiments, even when the going is slow and the path forward is uncertain. I am frequently reminded that Theodor Geisel, better known as Dr. Seuss, sent his first manuscript, *And to Think That I Saw It on Mulberry Street*, to twenty-seven publishers before one agreed to publish it. If he had not been persistent, and built on that first success, the world would have been denied his hugely popular collection of over sixty children's books.

- *What tiny spark can you create today?*
- *How will you add fuel to that tiny spark?*
- *What lucky breaks have resulted from building on tiny wins in your life?*

14

Capture Luck

Luck favors those who ask questions,
each one baiting good fortune to bite.

I was first introduced to David Eagleman's work when I read an article about him in *The New Yorker*.[1] The article was about his work trying to understand how time is measured by the brain. That question alone was fascinating. As a neuroscientist, I had never heard of someone trying to understand how the brain tracks time. The fact that it hadn't been done before didn't stop David. He was keen to figure out why some experiences, such as an accident, feel like they happen in slow motion, while others zip by quickly, soon to be forgotten. He learned through his research that the brain puts down many more memories during jarring experiences that are outside our normal existence, leading us to feel as though those events happened in slow motion.

After reading the article, I went down a rabbit hole of reading David's books, and my mind was blown by the diversity of projects that grabbed his attention. One was a short science fiction book he wrote called *Sum*, with forty chapters about what could happen to us when we die. Each chapter uses death as a window into a self-assessment of how we live our lives. The title story, "Sum," imagines that when we die, we live our life over again with each activity aggregated, so that we spend thirty years in a row sleeping, eighteen months waiting in line, and two hundred days in the shower, and so on.[2]

David's curiosity has opened doors to many more exciting opportunities. For example, *Sum* was turned into an opera. David was invited to develop a TV series on the brain, and to be the scientific advisor to the popular TV show *Westworld*. David recently launched an award-winning podcast about the brain called *Inner Cosmos*. Had he not asked provocative questions, such as what happens after we die, or how does the brain code for time, none of these opportunities would have materialized. David's luck has been the direct result of his curiosity.

After David arrived at Stanford in 2015, I reached out to introduce myself as his biggest fan. He graciously agreed to meet, and it quickly became clear that David's curiosity knows no bounds. In our conversations I learned that while his parents nurtured his inquisitive spirit, not all his teachers saw it as an asset. One advisor even warned him that his curiosity would get in the way of his success and that he would never amount to much unless he picked a single focus.

David ultimately discovered that depth and breadth aren't mutually exclusive. He realized that immersing himself in one discipline could give him the foundation to explore many others. It's like a tree: The deeper the roots, the farther the branches can spread. Neuroscience became David's roots, an intellectual anchor from which he could grow outward in countless directions.

This balance of depth and breadth has long intrigued psychologists. Over a century ago, early researchers began studying different forms of curiosity and their role in human survival. They found that curiosity fuels learning, drives problem-solving, sparks creativity, strengthens social bonds, and helps us adapt to a changing world.

Modern psychologists often distinguish between two types of curious minds: those who go deep and those who go wide. Deep divers focus intensely on a single subject, such as Roman history, modern art, or quantum mechanics, studying it from every angle until they become experts. The physicist Marie Curie exemplifies this approach, dedicating her life to understanding radioactivity, a pursuit that earned her two Nobel Prizes.

In contrast, wide explorers are driven by curiosity that resembles a searchlight rather than a laser beam. They scan a broad range of topics, making connections across disciplines and drawing insights from unexpected places. David Epstein explores the power of this approach in his book *Range*, where he highlights how breadth, not just depth, can be a competitive advantage in complex, rapidly changing environments.[3] One striking example is the naturalist Charles Darwin, whose transformative ideas about evolution were not the product of narrow specialization but of wide and patient observation. During his voyage on the HMS *Beagle*, Darwin studied geology, birds, barnacles, and ecosystems across continents. It was the interplay between these observations that ultimately led to his groundbreaking theory of natural selection. Wide explorers thrive at the edges, where disciplines blur. Their gift is connecting the dots. In doing so, they often redefine what's possible in their fields or create entirely new ones.

Some of the most innovative thinkers combine both modes, toggling between breadth and depth, flaring and focusing. The inventor Thomas Edison exemplified this blend. He cast a wide net when identifying problems worth solving, such as the light bulb, phonograph, and motion picture camera. Once he chose a challenge, he dove deep. In developing the light bulb, he ran thousands of experiments to find the perfect filament. As he famously said, "I have not failed. I've just found ten thousand ways that won't work."

I'm personally inspired by one of our students who has cultivated a longstanding curiosity practice. Rawan Dareer studied law at Stanford and is building a platform to search legal documents across Africa. Each week since she was a teenager, she has set aside a full day to explore something she knows little about. This might be a deep dive into the work of a single film director, the causes of the 2008 financial crisis, or the origins of fast food. The topic is always something she doesn't fully understand, a skill she wants to develop, or a person about whom she wants to learn more. This weekly practice began in childhood, sparked by Rawan's desire to answer the many questions she had about the world around her. Over time, it has become a powerful tool for self-discovery, helping Rawan identify the topics that resonate most deeply.

Successful companies understand the value of exploration and actively nurture employee curiosity in the pursuit of innovation and growth. Google became well known for its "20 percent time" policy, which encouraged employees to spend a portion of their workweek exploring new ideas driven by their interests. This freedom sparked the creation of major products like Gmail, AdSense, and Google News, all innovations that generated billions in revenue. The policy was especially valuable in Google's early years, when the company was exploring a wide range of possibilities aligned with its mission to organize the world's information. Over time, Google evolved this approach into more formalized innovation programs, helping to embed a culture of experimentation and creativity throughout the organization.

One of the most overlooked aspects of curiosity is one that can be practiced every day: listening. Not just hearing words but being fully present with another person and really listening to them. Giving someone your full attention helps you gain insights and unlocks connections. Listening is magnetic. It draws people toward you. When you listen with authentic curiosity, others feel it. They lean in and open up. That kind of presence builds trust, deepens relationships, and creates the kind of bonds that lead to unexpected opportunities.

But there's more. Curious listening helps you notice what others miss. A throwaway comment, a half-formed idea, a moment of hesitation can be a spark for new projects, partnerships, or insights if you're tuned in enough to catch them. To paraphrase the professional baseball player Yogi Berra, "You can observe a lot just by listening."

At Stanford Graduate School of Business, Debra Schifrin teaches her students that deep listening with authentic curiosity is one of the most powerful ways to make people feel truly seen and valued. When people feel heard, trust grows and the quality of collaboration skyrockets. The challenge? Most of us are so focused on what we're going to say next that we miss the chance in front of us.

Debra offers four simple but powerful ways to become a better listener:

- **Listen until the end of someone's story:** Don't interrupt—let the whole idea emerge.
- **Listen to summarize:** Before jumping in, reflect what you heard.

- **Listen to build the relationship:** Focus on the person, not just the content.
- **Listen for values:** What really matters to this person? What's underneath their words?

In her words, "Really listening elevates interactions into meaningful moments of growth and connection." And when you're truly curious, truly listening, luck shows up.[4] In *The Charisma Myth*, Olivia Fox Cabane says that you should be relentlessly curious and listen as though the person talking is the main character in a movie you are watching.[5]

The person I know who does this best is my friend and colleague Matt Abrahams, who has a successful podcast called *Think Fast, Talk Smart*. In his interviews, he always listens with the intent to summarize, following every one of his guest's comments with a short recap before asking the next question. He is a communication expert and knows that this approach makes his guests feel heard and heard correctly. Matt also recommends avoiding listening potholes that echo Debra's, such as just waiting for your turn to speak, but really focusing on the other person. To do this you need to identify and eliminate distracting physical noises in the environment; distracting psychological noises in your own mind, such as judgment or jealousy; and physiological noise in your body, such as hunger or exhaustion.

Curiosity is like casting a line into the unknown. Each question or observation you make increases your chances of reeling in a bit of luck. It pulls you into new places, sharpens what you notice, and inspires conversations others might overlook. Every inquiry becomes another cast, another chance to hook an unexpected insight or connection. Over time, curiosity broadens your network, expands your knowledge, and raises the odds of encountering unexpected good luck. Don't take my word for it. Theoretical physicist Albert Einstein credited much of his success not to innate brilliance but to his insatiable curiosity. As he famously said, "I have no special talent. I am only passionately curious."

- *Where will your curiosity take you?*
- *What questions will you ask that unlock new opportunities?*
- *What can you learn from listening more closely to those around you?*

15

Rebound to Luck

*Luck favors the resilient, who turn
setbacks into second chances.*

I was sure I was going to die. In a panic, I collapsed into a corner right outside my lab. Minutes earlier I had opened a cardboard package wrapped in masking tape that had been stored in our lab freezer down the hallway. The box contained tetrodotoxin (TTX), which is found in the ovaries of pufferfish. It is a potent sodium channel blocker that can kill you, and I needed it for my experiments to isolate potassium currents in the nerve cells I was studying.

After I peeled back the tape and opened the box, I found that all the TTX vials were open, and nothing was inside. It appeared that the contents had spilled out, and after a moment or two, I was convinced that I had been exposed to this extremely toxic poison. I started washing my hands over and over, and then when my heart started racing, I went into the hallway and melted into the corner, sure that something terrible was about to happen.

My fear subsided after a while. Much later, I concluded that the most likely explanation was that someone else had used the TTX, wrapped up the empty vials, and put them back in the freezer so that they could properly dispose of them later. Although I was physically fine, the fear remained, and it became impossible for me to do my research. Whenever I got near the lab I went into a panic.

This was not a recipe for successfully completing the lab work I needed to graduate. I therefore needed to find a way to bounce back. Armed with a bit of knowledge about behavior modification therapy, I decided to try it on myself with systematic desensitization. Over the course of many weeks, I got closer and closer to the lab, then closer and closer to the lab bench, and finally closer and closer to newly procured vials of TTX. Whenever I started feeling anxious, I stopped to drink some water very slowly and started walking toward the emergency room at the hospital, which was conveniently not too far from my laboratory. I never made it to the emergency room, but knowing it was there was a comfort. . . . With time, I was back in business and completed all my research experiments.

This experience taught me that bouncing back is possible. It took a change in both my attitude and actions. I needed to believe that I would be able to go back to the lab, and to physically move closer and closer to that goal. This demonstrated Friedrich Nietzsche's aphorism "What does not kill you makes you stronger."

Setbacks, like sudden storms, are part of every journey. What matters is how you respond. If you are resilient and readjust your sails, you stay open to what comes next, where luck is most likely to appear. But if you drop anchor and stop altogether, you risk missing an opportunity.

Resilience can be learned. In *The Resilience Factor*, Karen Reivich and Andrew Shatté describe specific skills that can be honed to build resilience in the face of inevitable setbacks in your life.[1] They describe seven skills that can be applied to manage tough situations that in the moment might feel intractable:

- Understanding and managing your feelings
- Slowing down to think rationally
- Taking a positive view of the situation
- Figuring out what is really going on
- Taking on different perspectives
- Understanding that you can impact the outcome
- Asking for help from others when needed.

Sometimes you don't have the luxury of time to slowly go through all these steps to bounce back. Instead, you must find a way to get over your fear or disappointment immediately. Think of gymnasts who perform under high pressure. After years of training and recovery from injuries, they have only a few minutes to stick the landing during a competition. If, one minute into their carefully crafted and practiced routine, they stumble, they must get back up and continue with grace. They practice their routines under extreme stress to exercise their resilience.

Tenaya West, a surgeon and former gymnast, shared how gymnasts train to literally bounce back from stumbles during a routine. First, each gymnast creates a mental routine that mirrors their physical routine. This means that when they trip or fall, they quickly use their mental routine to get them back into their physical routine. Second, they practice these routines every day so that they become ingrained. They say the words in their head, including trigger words for each movement, such as *core*, *arms*, or *breathe*, as positive affirmations. They repeat these words frequently, even while standing in line at the grocery store.

Gymnasts also learn how to keep going in the face of distractions, since they will certainly face unexpected disturbances during a competition, including buzzers, bells, cheers, and hisses. To prepare for this, the women's gymnastics team at Stanford might invite the men's volleyball team to heckle them while they practice, or to throw foam blocks at them during a complex routine so they learn to stay focused under difficult circumstances. Finally, when they finish a routine, whether it is perfect or not, the gymnasts learn to project a positive attitude to help the entire team stay upbeat. Tenaya told me that this intense resilience training spills into other aspects of her life as well, leading to more generalized resilience. As a medical resident learning surgery, she was able to bounce back quickly when given corrective feedback, and to switch gears rapidly when a complicated surgical case requires a new strategy.

It is critical to acknowledge to yourself that obstacles are to be expected. Even if you can't predict exactly what or when disappointments will arise, you can prepare yourself by strengthening your resilience. One of the most effective ways to build resilience is by framing failure as a learning experience. I'm a fan of keeping a failure résumé. This is the opposite of your traditional list of achievements. It's an inventory of your mess-ups, disappointments, and setbacks—personal, professional, and academic—and the lessons learned from each one. By taking the time to acknowledge mistakes, what you learned from them, and what you will do differently the next time, you are much less likely to repeat them. You are also less likely to perseverate, continuing to stew on errors long after they happened.

Matt Abrahams, mentioned in the prior chapter, teaches at Stanford's business school. He told me about a company for which he worked that celebrated learning from failure by hosting Failure Friday each week. Everyone in the company got up at the end of the week to share their biggest mess-ups. The one voted the biggest failure was awarded a small cash prize, enough for a dinner date. The catch was that you couldn't get the prize twice for the same mistake. The assumption was that everyone would learn from their error, and it wouldn't happen again. For example, Matt received the prize for planning a sales conference in August in Europe, making all the arrangements, including buying plane tickets and printing slogans on T-shirts, only to learn that most of the people they wanted to attend would be on vacation at that time. Oops! Although they were out a few thousand dollars after unwinding the effort, nobody on the team made the same mistake again!

Every entry on your failure résumé tells a story of growth. It's a reminder that failure isn't the end of the road but a stepping stone on the path to success. By revisiting these moments, you can see how much you've already overcome and how each misstep has shaped your journey. This practice not only reinforces your ability to recover but also builds confidence that you can handle future obstacles, no matter how daunting they may seem. After all, resilience isn't about avoiding failure but rather knowing that you have the tools to recover.

Resilience is essential not only when you actively pursue challenges but also when you are subjected to circumstances beyond your control. The story that Roya shared with me took my breath away as she recounted all the obstacles she faced on her journey from a rural district in Afghanistan to college in New York City, and then to Stanford. The journey called upon her relentless resilience to recover from wave upon wave of obstacles placed in her path.

Roya (not her real name) was born in Herat, more than a thousand kilometers from Kabul, the capital. The fourth of five siblings, Roya was raised by her strict uncle after the Taliban killed her father. Their home housed twenty-four family members, and Roya's immediate family of six shared a single small room. The rules for women were suffocating. They were forbidden to speak in the presence of men and required to always wear a headscarf. She wasn't allowed to visit relatives or friends, so school was her only refuge. There, she secretly studied English, even though her future seemed predetermined. She was expected to marry one of her cousins after graduation and remain in the same household to raise a family.

At the risk of being disowned, Roya defied expectations and took the entrance exam for the American University of Afghanistan in Kabul. To her amazement, she was accepted with a much-needed scholarship. But telling her uncle was terrifying. When her brother cautiously raised the subject, her uncle's response was an immediate and explosive "No!" He warned that if she left for Kabul, she would not be welcome back. It was a one-way ticket.

She chose the one-way ticket.

Having never even visited her local town of Herat, let alone a city as vast as Kabul, Roya found the move overwhelming. For two months, she cried, fearing she had made the wrong decision. But a phone call with her brother reminded her why she had fought for this opportunity. Determined, she redoubled her focus on her studies. At the same time, she took on a job to send money home because her mother and siblings had been thrown out of her uncle's house when he discovered that her brother had supported her decision to go to college.

As Roya's ambitions grew, she applied to transfer to Baruch College in New York City. When she was accepted, she sent her passport to the embassy to secure a visa. But just as her dreams were within reach, the world around her collapsed. The United States withdrew from Afghanistan, the Taliban seized power, and the government disintegrated overnight.

Once again, Roya had to find a way forward. She rushed to the bank to withdraw her savings, only to be told there was no money. She then learned that all passports had been destroyed. Knowing the US was helping some Afghans escape, she made daily trips to the airport, hoping to be chosen. Alongside thousands of others, she slept outside the gates, going days without food or water. After a week of futile attempts, she tried the Pakistan border only to find it closed.

Eventually Roya connected with US veterans working in Kabul to help people flee. She persuaded them to add her name to a list for transport out of the country, and then she waited. Two months passed before she finally received a call. That call led to a flight to Abu Dhabi, where she endured another long wait for a student visa.

Finally, in January 2022, Roya's visa was approved. Her journey to New York took several days, with multiple stops along the way. When she landed, she had no idea where to go or what to do. A thoughtful Afghan friend she had met online arranged a short-term rental for her, and observant students at Baruch College, seeing her shivering in the brutal New York winter, found her a jacket. Despite the hardships, and despite being uprooted time and again, Roya persevered and learned how to bounce back every time she was disappointed. She rebuilt her life over and over and over again, recovering from all the world was throwing at her. Roya is now studying law at Stanford and dreams of using her developing knowledge and skills to help others like her who are striving to live in peace and freedom.

Challenges, failures, and disappointments are a natural part of life, and sometimes they feel existential. Nobody gets away without them. They can be like a slowly approaching tsunami, giving you plenty of time to get out of the way; or like an earthquake that shakes your foundation without warning. Either way, they test your resilience and adaptability. The key is understanding that resilience from setbacks is a skill that can be learned and honed. Just as seasoned sailors learn to read the wind and waves, adjusting their course when storms arise, you, too, can develop the ability to adapt to life's uncertainties and disappointments. Resilience is more than recovery; it's a force multiplier for luck. Each time you rise again from a setback, you stay in the game and have another opportunity to try again.

- *Where have you shown the most resilience?*
- *What can you do to enhance your ability to bounce back?*
- *What have been lucky benefits of strengthening your resilience?*

16

Invent Luck

Luck favors those who see problems as opportunities for a creative solution.

When the pandemic hit in March 2020, Katherine Emery's world and work collapsed. Not only did her photography business in San Francisco dry up but she was also caring for a family member with a frightening illness. With everything falling apart, she and her family made the courageous decision to pick up and move across the country to Mount Desert Island, Maine, her husband's hometown, to get a fresh start.

Katherine had to build her photography business anew, but due to pandemic restrictions, it was nearly impossible to meet potential clients in person. Katherine felt like an island on an island.

Feeling the pressure to start all over again, Katherine needed to tap into her creativity to find a way forward. This involved defining the problem, embracing the constraints, challenging assumptions, generating solutions, including crazy ideas, and testing them to see what worked. These are the hallmarks of creative problem-solving that can be used to turn challenges into opportunities, unlocking lucky breaks.

Katherine started by making lists: lists of photo documentaries she wanted to produce, lists of fine art projects she wanted to develop, and potential professional work that would pay the bills. Diving deeper, she listed seven organizations in the local community with which she would be delighted to work, including family foundations, land trusts, and a research institute. The big question was how to make contacts with these groups, since Katherine was new to the community and knew nobody.

Katherine decided to start small... really small. She set up pop-up portrait stations where anyone in the Mount Desert Island community could get a professional portrait for only fifty dollars. She received permission from two community centers and one restaurant to set up a station to take photos and offered free photos to anyone who worked in those organizations. She also offered to donate one free photo to a local nonprofit for every paid portrait. Katherine's goal was to find ways to quickly contribute to the community and start building trusting relationships. She knew that those relationships would be the key to future opportunities, as discussed in chapter 9.

Katherine soon learned that community members were keen to have professional photos taken and were thrilled by the images that Katherine created. Word-of-mouth referrals began to spread, and Katherine then built on that success by crafting an email introducing herself and her work, including a handful of beautiful photos. The email also included an offer for a free portrait. She sent it to the parents of her daughter's classmates, who were the only people she knew in town. Within a few days, forty-two people signed up for portraits, and word about Katherine's business began to spread.

Katherine took photos of teachers, a mother and child, four business owners, the president of a local college, a lawyer, a former diplomat, two writers, four artists, and a fisherman who had never had a portrait taken. She asked each person how they heard about the photo shoot and learned who in the community was responsible for spreading the word. She thanked her advocates profusely, an important step, as discussed in chapter 7.

Serendipitously, at the same time, a local nonprofit was on the hunt for a professional photographer and shared their quest on a community online forum. Nine of the people whom Katherine had photographed recommended her for the job! A couple of weeks later, in late May, Katherine received calls from five local organizations inquiring about using her services for their projects. All five were on the list of dream clients she had compiled.

The tiny seeds that Katherine planted took root, sprouted, and grew into a flourishing business. Since the day she offered portraits for fifty dollars, only two months before, she had been commissioned to make photos for editorial magazines, nonprofits, and small businesses needing visual branding, as well as family reunions, weddings, graduations, and even fishing boats. No advertising required—it was all word of mouth.

This story is a powerful reminder that the winds of luck are abundant, but you won't catch them without building your ship, recruiting your crew, and hoisting your sail. Katherine did this by tapping into her creative problem-solving skills to clearly define the problem (how to build awareness for her business), embracing her constraints (she didn't know anyone in the community), challenging assumptions about generally accepted ways to build a new business (advertising versus word of mouth), identifying target organizations (revising as she went along), and testing her ideas (even the seemingly crazy ones).

Constraints, such as those that Katherine faced, can serve as powerful catalysts for creative thinking. These constraints come in different flavors:

- **Input constraints**—working with what you've got. In Katherine's case, she was constrained by not knowing anyone in her new community.
- **Process constraints**—reimagining how things get done. For Katherine, this was a lack of funds to pay for advertisements or rent a photo studio.

- **Output constraints**—identifying needed outcomes.
  Katherine focused on the unique needs of her community
  by offering professional headshots instead of, say, fine art
  projects.

Sometimes the most interesting and effective solutions to problems emerge not from having unlimited resources but from the creative tension that results from working within well-defined boundaries. The pandemic lockdown, with all its limitations, served as a fertile stimulant for rethinking almost everything. These constraints emerged quickly and had a direct and immediate effect on those of us who teach.

It was Friday, March 13, 2020, and the world shut down. I got a haircut that afternoon, thinking I would zip back to campus afterward. Instead, the campus closed, and I wouldn't set foot in a classroom again for nearly two years. As an educator I had some big decisions to make: Do I continue to teach the way I did before the lockdown or do I find new ways to teach? I chose to find the opportunities in the new upside-down world. As someone who teaches creative problem-solving, it was the only option.

First, I realized that many of my students had lost internships and were panicked about what they would do that summer. So, I quickly designed a virtual summer internship program with my colleagues at the Stanford Technology Ventures Program (STVP). We offered eighty students the chance to work remotely and curate collections from

STVP's vast repository of eCorner online videos. Additionally, we hosted weekly online lectures and discussions about entrepreneurship. The result was that the students had an engaging summer experience and STVP wound up with a valuable set of online collections.

Second, I experimented with an online course that was open to anyone in the world, using a concept I called "Jolts."[1] Every day for thirty days I ran a "byte-size" class on Twitter consisting of a short video clip and a brief assignment. Other organizations created similar opportunities for the community. The Getty Museum launched an art challenge in March 2020,[2] during the lockdown, prompting everyone to recreate their favorite artwork with things they had around the house. The results were astonishing! Using kitchen utensils, packaged food, and other household items, people around the world used their ingenuity to recreate great works of art. My friends and I tried our hand at this, too, with playful new renditions of Vincent van Gogh's sunflowers, Frida Kahlo's self-portrait, Michelangelo's *The Creation of Adam*, and Wayne Thiebaud's desserts.

I had some experience teaching with constraints when I delivered courses on entrepreneurship to the men in The Last Mile program at San Quentin State Prison. The men in my courses had to complete assignments using the limited resources they had on hand. One year, the team project focused on addressing needs related to local wildfires, a topic that was very close to their hearts because the San Francisco

Bay Area fires engulfed the prison in thick smoke. Plus, many of the men worked on the front lines of the fires alongside professional fire fighters.

During the course, the men identified problems related to wildfires, such as prevention and evacuation, then brainstormed about possible solutions, and finally tested those ideas with those around them. I then challenged the men to create a short video to pitch their idea. When I first mentioned the video, the men looked at me with confusion and concern. How were they supposed to make a video in prison? They didn't have cameras or video editing equipment. I knew that the men had access to computers because they all took software coding classes, so I smiled and said, "Creativity loves constraints. I'm sure you will figure it out. I'll see you again in two weeks for the presentations."

Two weeks passed, and when I arrived back at San Quentin, I had no idea what I would find. The videos were incredible! The men had figured out how to use the computer-based tools that they had to create some of the most remarkable and moving videos I have seen in any of my classes. Not only did the men learn how to make videos that told compelling stories but they also learned that constraints can be a tangible stimulant for creative problem-solving.

The mental flexibility to see limitations as a launchpad for creativity is valuable far beyond extreme environments and crisis management. It frees you to tap into all the resources you have around you instead of lamenting what you're missing. This mindset, in conjunction with other creative problem-solving tools discussed above, is among the most important factors in unlocking luck. It enables you to identify solutions to problems that might stall someone else. Instead of feeling stuck in the doldrums, creativity allows you to reframe challenges as opportunities, adapt quickly to new circumstances, and chart paths around obstacles, often leading to outcomes that at first seemed impossible.

This is exactly what Danit Peleg did. While in school in Israel to become a fashion designer, Danit decided that she wanted to try her hand at creating a line of soft clothing made entirely with 3D printing. Her professors told her that it was impossible, especially with the tight time constraint of completing the project in only nine months. Undeterred, Danit decided to dive in despite her limited time, limited knowledge, limited support, and even more limited budget. This was 2015, when there was virtually no information about 3D-printed fashion or textiles available.

She started with what she did have—drive, determination, and creativity. Unable to afford the printers, she approached a local reseller and proposed a barter. If he lent her six desktop 3D printers for the nine-month project, she would create a fashion photo of a 3D-printed dress that he could feature in his marketing materials. He agreed, and within days the six machines were humming in her living room.

Next, Danit tackled the "fabric" problem. Typical 3D-printed materials aren't soft enough for clothing. She didn't let this slow her down, experimenting until she found a newly developed, ultra-flexible filament available from a supplier in Spain. Danit sent the supplier a photo of a red biker jacket, her first full-size garment she made using this material. The supplier was so impressed that he sent her a free box of spools to complete her collection.

The next step was finding a pattern for her fabric. Extensive searching led Danit to an architect's open-source design, which she repurposed to look like lace by changing the scale and density of the pattern. A few weeks later, her printers were spinning out lacy fabric panels, and Danit was able to complete her project. At the fashion show at the end of the year, she debuted her collection of 100 percent 3D-printed outfits, including skirts, dresses, a jacket, shoes, and accessories in multiple colors.

While working on this project, Danit's husband documented the process, taking photos and making videos that he posted online. The content was picked up by press from around the world. The waves of impact continue to unfold. Ten years on, Danit has exchanged the borrowed printers for custom printers, and she turns scraps from fashion and sneaker factories into fresh filament for beautiful new clothes. Danit is still pushing the boundaries and is working with companies across industries who are eager to learn from her.[3] Talking to Danit about her journey, she reflects, "The severe constraints gave me tunnel vision on my goals. This focus turned what was seemingly impossible into something inevitable."

Luck is often a direct result of looking at challenges as opportunities. In so many ways, the biggest problems are the biggest opportunities! Many of the world's most successful ventures were born not from ideal circumstances but in response to obstacles that demanded a novel response. Constraints force creativity, and adversity can sharpen focus. When you meet difficulty with determination and an open mind, you create the conditions for luck to emerge.

- *What problems in your life are opportunities in disguise?*
- *What constraints will you mine for creative solutions?*
- *How will you unlock luck hidden in challenges?*

17

Prioritize Luck

*Luck favors those who say no, clearing
clutter from the road to success.*

When Drew Endy landed his first professional job in 2002, he was fired up and ready to make an impact. He sketched out a long list of ambitious goals, eager to hit the ground running. But by the end of his first week, reality hit. He hadn't accomplished one. Instead, his entire week had been consumed with meetings.

Frustrated, Drew turned to a mentor, who nodded kindly and said, "Oh, yes, that's normal. You need to learn to say no. There will always be endless distractions." Determined to take control, Drew grabbed a huge marker, scrawled "NO" in bold letters on a large piece of paper, and taped it on the wall in front of his desk. Problem solved, right? Maybe . . . for about six months.

Before long, the cycle repeated. Drew's schedule overflowed with commitments based on other people's priorities, not his own. Once again, Drew felt himself falling behind. So, he went back to his mentor. "That happens," the mentor said. "You need to get better at saying no."

Drew needed a new strategy, and this time he got more creative. He started responding to requests with this phrase: "Great idea! Let's work on it together . . . in the future." To reinforce his commitment to saying no, he attached a spring to his phone cord, so it was always trying to hang up the phone. That served as a physical reminder to keep calls short and focused, and the tactic bought him another six months of productivity.

Then it happened again. Drew, drowning in obligations once again, was going to turn to his mentor for a third time but stopped short. He knew what his mentor would say: "You need to get even better at saying no."

Drew pondered this for a while and then realized that he hated saying no. Instead, he loved to say yes! The path his well-intentioned mentor had set him on was an endless future of finding more clever ways to say no. So Drew pivoted to saying yes only to new opportunities that aligned with his own goals. This made it much easier to say no.

Knowing when to say yes and when to say no allows you to allocate your time and energy. Saying yes commits you, and saying no protects your time for something else. It is easy to say yes. But saying no politely is a skill, especially when you want to keep the door open in the future. You don't want to burn bridges that you may want to cross in the future. Here are some responses that I've found work well:

- Thank you so much for the opportunity. Unfortunately I can't participate right now given my other commitments. Please feel free to ask again in the future. *This polite response keeps the door open for future opportunities.*
- Unfortunately, I am not able to participate, but I am happy to recommend someone else. *This directs the opportunity to someone who may be delighted by the referral.*
- I don't have time to meet. Please feel free to send me one or two questions via email, and I will do my best to answer them. *This response allows you to help to the level you feel comfortable.*
- What an interesting project. Unfortunately it is not my area of expertise. *This response is a gracious way to respond to a request that doesn't match your skills, interests, or abilities.*

Keep in mind that saying no quickly and politely is helpful to both you and the recipient. It doesn't leave them hanging, waiting for a response; and it gets the request off your plate. If you say yes initially and then subsequently cancel at the last minute, it leaves a bad impression and may put the other party in a difficult predicament if they can't find a last-minute replacement. A quick and clear no is a gift.

Now you might think that saying no conflicts with the concept of injecting randomness, which I covered in chapter 11. Yes, you should be open to new opportunities, but not at the expense of the things that matter most to you. If you are training to run a marathon, you need to carve out time to train every day and protect that time in your schedule. Similarly, if you are preparing for an exam, you need to make time to study. Saying no prevents diversions away from your primary objectives.

Make a commitment to "decide to decide" what is important to you, and then map your time to match those goals. In a world full of distractions and competing demands, clarity is a superpower. Without it, we react rather than choose. The historian and author Will Durant captured Aristotle's thoughts on this when he wrote, "We are what we repeatedly do," in his 1926 book *The Story of Philosophy*.[1] In other words, your calendar is a mirror of your true commitments. When you say no to something, you are saying yes to something else. There are only twenty-four hours in the day, and you must rank how you spend them. If you don't prioritize your time, it will be frittered away. As the business strategist Greg McKeown writes in *Essentialism*,[2] "Choosing not to choose is also a choice—one that will allow others to make your decisions for you."

Research by the marketing professors Julian Givi and Colleen P. Kirk shows that we overestimate the impact of saying no. Their research with more than two thousand participants showed the impact of saying no to an invitation was much less consequential than expected.[3] "Across our experiments, we consistently found that invitees overestimate the negative ramifications that arise in the eyes of inviters following an invitation decline," Givi said.[4] Therefore, you shouldn't be obliged to say yes when you really want to say no.

The importance of saying no became crystal clear to Piya Sorcar, introduced in chapter 6. Piya is the driving force behind TeachAids, a nonprofit she founded in 2009 to create educational tools to prevent HIV and then later to combat concussions in student athletes. For years, Piya poured herself into these missions, working twelve-to-fourteen-hour days to reach millions of people across the globe. She couldn't keep operating at full speed forever, so Piya pulled her sailboat out of the water for repairs. She needed time to recover before diving back in to pursue her next mission.

Rest isn't a retreat; it's a strategy for success. Knowing when to go full speed ahead and when to dock for maintenance will help sustain long-term success. Sometimes, as Drew Endy learned, the most powerful yes is the one you give to yourself.

There are times when it isn't clear when to say yes or no to an opportunity. In these scenarios, decision science can provide a clue. Mykel Kochenderfer studies decision-making under uncertainty. His research shows that when the outcome of a situation is uncertain, you want to say yes more frequently at the beginning of the process so you can explore the landscape of possibilities. Think of being a freshman in college who is encouraged to take lots of different courses to see what sparks their interest. This is the "flare" stage, when you say yes to everything. Then once you find something that grabs you, it's time to focus and switch to exploitation by saying no to distractions. Using the metaphor I introduced at the beginning of this book, flaring happens when you are a hot-air balloon, exploring the world of possibilities. Focusing happens when you're a windmill or a sailboat, switching to actively harnessing and seeking out luck.

There is a classic decision-making problem that first appeared in print in 1960, known variously as the secretary problem, the marriage problem, or the best choice problem. Although the names are dated, the concept explores a fundamental question: How long should you spend exploring options (flaring) before committing to a decision (focusing)?

Mathematicians have an optimal strategy: Spend the first 37 percent of your time evaluating options without committing to any of them. If you're choosing an apartment or making any decision where options arrive sequentially, this initial period sets a benchmark for what the ideal solution would be. Thereafter, you should only select a new apartment that is better than any of the others you've seen up to that point. This approach maximizes your chances of making the best possible choice.

Here's how it works in practice. Say you are moving to a new city and plan to see ten apartments over the next two weeks. According to the 37 percent rule, you should visit three or four apartments (37 percent of ten) without any intention to commit. After that, use those visits to set a baseline, now knowing what is typical given your budget and location. Then starting with the fifth apartment, pick the first one that is better than any of the first four. This works because you are giving yourself enough exposure to learn what is available, but you aren't waiting so long that you miss out on the best option.

We can summarize the process in a simple decision-making rule set:

- Flare for 37 percent of the time—gather data, explore possibilities.
- Then focus and commit when the right opportunity arises.

This balance of exploration and exploitation helps you navigate the trade-offs between seizing opportunities too soon and waiting too long and missing out.

Learning when and how to say no is a fundamental tool you need to perfect because it will protect your time, energy, and focus. In a world that constantly pushes us to say yes to every opportunity, request, or obligation, mastering the art of strategic refusal is what separates those who are merely busy from those who are ultimately lucky. Saying no isn't about shutting doors; it's about keeping the right ones open.

The luckiest people aren't the ones who do the most; they're the ones who choose what to do most wisely.

- *Have you decided to decide on your priorities?*
- *What will you turn down to focus on what is most important to you right now?*
- *What lucky opportunities emerge when you clear your life of clutter?*

18

Stretch Toward Luck

Luck favors those who embrace imposter syndrome, as fortune forms at the frontier.

The week before his first classes were to start, Matt Abrahams walked into the room for a half-day training for new lecturers at the Stanford Graduate School of Business and was decidedly intimidated. He felt like an imposter with so many notable people in the room, many of whom were titans of industry and well-known experts in the corporate world. Having taught at a community college for many years, Matt was concerned that others might see him as a fish out of water.

As the day progressed, it became clear that while many of the people around the table clearly knew how to run global businesses, many had never taught before. Some of the participants asked questions that Matt knew how to answer. For example, how do you teach students when some are nonnative English speakers? Matt was quick to jump in, based on his experience and expertise, and encouraged them to use the "think, pair, share" model of teaching. The model gives students time to think about the prompt independently and then pair up with other students to discuss further among themselves, and then together with the entire class. This approach gives everyone time to collect their thoughts before the discussion phase. Matt's workshop attendees found this technique very insightful, and Matt realized that he wasn't an imposter after all but, instead, fit right in.

Imposter syndrome is a topic Matt now addresses frequently in his classes on public speaking, where it's a concern of many students. His message to those who feel inadequate and unprepared to speak is that fear of public speaking is normal. The trick is figuring out how to move past those feelings so that you don't throw away the opportunity to share your ideas publicly. Sharing, after all, is one of the most effective ways to increase luck, by asking for what you want.

The easiest way to overcome this fear is to address the sources and symptoms of imposter syndrome. The sources are often the fear of making a mistake or anxiety about the consequences of a bad performance. The symptoms can include dry mouth, sweaty palms, and a rapid heart rate. To overcome these issues, Matt suggests staying in the present by listening to music versus projecting yourself into the future where you imagine potential mistakes. He also recommends tricks to address physical symptoms of imposter syndrome, such as taking deep breaths, drinking water slowly, shaking out the energy, and holding a cold drink in your hand to cool down your body.

The pervasiveness of imposter syndrome was driven home to Matt when he was at the airport several years ago. A man approached him and asked if he wrote the book *Speaking Up without Freaking Out*.[1] Matt said he was the author, and the man confided that he had the book, had not read it, and that it had helped him enormously. Confused, Matt asked how the book helped him if he hadn't read it. With pride the man responded that the existence of a book on this topic made him realize that his fear of public speaking wasn't unique, so he decided to conquer it himself.

Matt shared other truths about imposter syndrome. As someone who has studied martial arts since he was a teenager, Matt has repeatedly been tested on his way to a third-level black belt in karate. Before his first black-belt test, Matt was anxious that he was an imposter and wouldn't perform well. A friend, knowing the test was imminent, told him to "have fun!" This comment threw him. How could a test possibly be fun? Matt pondered this a bit and then shifted his perspective to see that this opportunity could be fun. He was prepared and had nothing to fear. He subsequently crushed the test. As the writer Suzy Kassem says, "Doubt kills more dreams than failure ever will."[2]

Matt continues his martial arts training, and his coach—an eighth-degree black belt—often tells him that he is executing a move "correctly but in the wrong way." At first, this sounds paradoxical. How can something be both right and wrong? The coach's point is that while the outcome may look fine, the intentionality behind the movement is missing and its absence compromises the execution. In martial arts, as in life, intention is discernible, and it matters.

There's a difference between reacting and responding, Matt learned. In his karate practice, he was reacting instead of performing with deliberate intention. When you anchor yourself with clear intentions, your actions become purposeful, executed with greater confidence, and more adaptable to changing circumstances. When you are clear on what you want to accomplish, your doubts fade into the background, so confidence can take center stage. The lesson here is that if you can anchor your behavior with your clear intentions, it will be more authentic and effective.

Imposter syndrome is so common because we are all faking it all the time. Life is improvisation. We aren't given a script for each day, and there are endless ways to succeed and fail with each interaction. That is why we need to embrace all circumstances by first being clear on our goals. Clarity lets us improvise and adapt to whatever comes our way by keeping our target in sight. Imposter syndrome could, in fact, be redefined as "improvement syndrome" since confidently stretching outside our comfort zone leads to growth.

A recent systematic review of imposter syndrome found that 82 percent of the fourteen thousand people surveyed experienced imposter syndrome at some point in their lives.[3]

It is equally prevalent across all age groups and is equally common in men and women. Unfortunately, its effects can be profoundly negative. The researchers found strong correlations between imposter syndrome and high levels of depression, anxiety, and low self-esteem, all which contribute to chronic stress and burnout.

On the flip side, there are benefits of imposter syndrome. First, it can lead to humility, because feeling like an imposter takes you down a notch. We are rarely the smartest person in every room, so humility is warranted. With humility comes a willingness to listen more and speak less.

Second, imposter syndrome can also motivate you to work harder to succeed. When you feel like an imposter, you tell yourself that you need to put in more effort to avoid failure. When you become complacent and think you can "phone it in" by doing the minimum amount, you lose your edge. Imposter syndrome is like a hand on the small of your back pushing you to try harder, to be better, and to achieve more.

Third, imposter syndrome can also lead to better collaboration. If you feel like an imposter, you are much more likely to ask questions and collaborate with others. When I begin teaching a course on a topic that's new to me, for example, I understand that feeling like an imposter is natural. Therefore, to combat this, my first step is always to find co-instructors and guest speakers who can fill the gaps in my knowledge. This inevitably leads to much better outcomes than if I tried to do it solo. Over time, as my knowledge and experience grow, I can put down some of those guardrails.

Finally, putting yourself in situations where you feel like an imposter is a courageous act that widens the aperture for lucky breaks. Every time you take on a challenge that stretches you beyond your comfort zone, you build the confidence to face future hurdles and increase your exposure to unexpected opportunities. Over time, you come to realize that the fear of failure is often far worse than the reality and that discomfort is a sign of growth, not inadequacy. When you reframe fear as courage, you learn to stand tall in the face of uncertainty. To push past imposter syndrome, take a cue from this well-known adage, often attributed to Eleanor Roosevelt, "Do one thing every day that scares you."

- *When has imposter syndrome held you back?*
- *How can you harness it to create lucky outcomes?*
- *What luck has resulted from stretching beyond your comfort zone?*

Conclusion

Luck Is a Long Game

T he trip was nearly a complete disaster. Along with about ten other families, we embarked on what we thought would be a relaxing getaway to Costa Rica, only to find it was the exact opposite of what we had envisioned. The trip organizers had scouted the hotels during the low season, when everything appeared calm and idyllic. Unfortunately our actual visit coincided with winter break, transforming the resort into a hot spot for college students ready to party.

The once tranquil pool now featured a floating bar, and the atmosphere was anything but serene. Bikini-clad revelers filled the area, and loud music pulsed through the hotel day and night. To make matters worse, the local drinking age was eighteen and barely enforced, which meant that our teenagers, many of whom were close to that age, had easy access to free-flowing alcohol. The hotel's beachfront location, while stunning, only added to our concerns, creating a worrisome mix of unsupervised partying, underage drinking, and a long list of other dangers. Parents found themselves on high alert, more focused on managing risks than enjoying the vacation we had all anticipated.

So, what to do? Some parents made a real scene and demanded their money back, while others jumped on a plane and got out of there. The trip program team on the ground, led by Deborah, were beside themselves doing whatever they could to rectify the situation in real time. They hadn't planned the trip but were now responsible for how it unfolded, and they were doing their best in a very difficult situation. Although frustrated and concerned, I talked with the staff and acknowledged that they were in a rough spot. We made it home unscathed and had a story to tell about the trip that went south, literally and figuratively!

Fast-forward fifteen years. I was being considered for my current role at Knight-Hennessy Scholars, and Deborah was now on the team evaluating me. I didn't recall that she had led the trip so many years before, but she surely remembered me. She didn't bring up the connection until long after I was hired. When she did, she confided that the trip had been a nightmare for her and reminded me how much she had appreciated the way I handled a disappointing situation. To be honest, I didn't remember that part either. What I do know is this: If I had behaved poorly fifteen years earlier, I wouldn't have been offered the job. It would have slipped through my fingers and I would never have known why.

This type of scenario happens all the time. Life is a long

game, and the choices you make today shape the opportunities that will come your way tomorrow. The world is surprisingly small. Just when you least expect it, you find yourself crossing paths with the same people, sometimes in the most unexpected places. When I see people acting badly, my first instinct is to think about how this behavior will reverberate in ways that they can't even imagine.

I recently shared this idea with Grace Isford, who is mentioned in chapter 8 on helping others. She had a relevant example of this principle in action. While walking down a street in San Francisco, she ran into someone with whom she had gone to high school in Connecticut many years earlier. They hadn't spoken in years, but her former classmate warmly reminded her of how kind Grace had been to her when she first moved to town. As the conversation unfolded, Grace learned that her old friend was now working at a company of interest to Grace. By the end of their sidewalk chat, her old acquaintance offered to make a valuable introduction at the company.

It was a moment of serendipity, but one that was possible only because of Grace's kindness years earlier. Had Grace treated her former classmate poorly back then, the outcome would certainly have been different. In fact, her old classmate might have crossed the street to avoid her instead! The lesson is clear: The way you show up in the world today will ripple forward in ways you can't predict, enabling or blocking future opportunities.

Good luck often begets more good luck precisely because positive interactions lead to future opportunities. Simply, if you treat someone well, they are much more likely to treat you well in the future. If, on the other hand, you act poorly, the likelihood that someone will want to help you in the future declines precipitously. Since luck so often stems from interactions with others, the results are inevitable.

Positive interactions are amplified over time, leading to increased lucky outcomes. This is supported by Robert Cialdini's research on reciprocity, discussed in his book *Influence*.[1] He shares how reciprocity is found across cultures and from the dawn of civilization, evolving as an important survival mechanism. Returned favors can come at any time, sometimes immediately and sometimes years or decades later. Interestingly, reciprocal favors are often asymmetrical, and a small initial favor may yield a much greater act of kindness in the future. For example, if you help someone with a math assignment in college, they might help you find a job years later. Consistent generosity to others weaves a wide web of goodwill and, like a progressively larger sail, eventually leads to more serendipitous opportunities in the future.

Just as good luck begets more good luck over time, bad luck does the same. When things turn south, it is common to retrench to avoid future disappointments and failures. The psychologist Martin Seligman described this as learned helplessness in which those with repeated disappointments develop belief that they have no control over their future.[2]

Loss of control decreases motivation and, in turn, effort, reinforcing a cycle of disappointments.[3]

It takes a concerted effort to turn things around. Effective strategies include developing a growth mindset, looking at setbacks as learning opportunities, focusing on tiny wins to help reverse a negative trend, and tapping into friendships to help you escape a downward spiral. Seligman captured these ideas in his book *Learned Optimism*,[4] an antidote to his book *Helplessness*,[5] in which he lays out specific tools to reverse the cycle of negative thinking. Seligman created a process for learning to be optimistic using an ABCDE mnemonic:

A. Recognize the **adversity**.
B. Identify your automatic **beliefs**.
C. Notice the **consequences** of those beliefs.
D. **Disrupt** that thought pattern; and
E. **Energize** a different pattern of thinking.

Seligman concluded that those with learned optimism are luckier specifically because they can bounce back from failures and create the conditions for future positive opportunities.

It is never too late to patch your sail and hoist it high to catch the winds of luck. Life is an open sea with endless horizons, and you can set out on your journey at any time and from anywhere. My father, nearly one hundred years old, is a living testament to this truth. Every day, he invites luck by adding fresh inputs into his life by reading widely, attending lectures, and staying intellectually curious. He is incredibly fortunate to be so vital at this stage of his life. He continues to hone good luck by practicing resilience as he navigates the evolving challenges of aging, never losing sight of what matters most. What stands out is how he celebrates those who support him. He expresses gratitude freely, creating a current of goodwill that flows back to him.

My father, without a doubt, remains one of the luckiest people I know. As described in the opening story of this book, he was incredibly fortunate to leave Nazi Germany in 1934, escaping what would have inevitably happened to his family had they stayed. He was eight years old, and his family arrived in the United States with practically nothing. They were so poor that my father couldn't live with his family, staying instead with his Uncle Leo's family with whom he couldn't easily communicate since he only spoke German at the time. He worked diligently to learn English and to excel in school. As I was growing up, he frequently reminded me that "the harder he worked, the luckier he got."

As his life unfolded, my father was fortunate to be at a party where he met my mother, and lucky enough to woo her successfully by writing daily letters when they were apart. He counts that as the luckiest part of his life, as she was the center of his world. Professionally, my father found himself at the right place at the right time (how fortunate) and was able to capitalize on those opportunities (how lucky). He frequently tells the story about the time his highly competent boss left to take another job, and my father was asked to fill that role, starting his journey as a manager. We continue to debate how much of it was fortune and how much of it was luck. He claims it happened *to him*, and I claim that he put himself in the position to be the obvious replacement for his boss.

As his career progressed, my father also weathered professional storms, the most crushing of which was getting fired while at the top of his career for entertaining a potential job offer from a competing firm. His boss required fierce loyalty, and when he learned that my father was considering a move, he forced him out. The hypothetical role never materialized when the other company reorganized and didn't hire anyone for the job. My father eventually bounced back and reinvented his career as an educator, teaching college courses on business and leadership, which was deeply satisfying to him.

Thirty-six years ago, while on a trip to Europe with my mother, my father suffered a serious heart attack. It happened while they were waltzing at an event in Vienna. It is his favorite music and one of his greatest joys. Life suddenly turned precarious, but fortune was on his side. The medication he urgently needed had been approved in Europe, though it was not yet available in the United States. The timing, the place, the access to effective treatment were all out of his control, and those factors made all the difference. After several weeks in the hospital, my father returned home and made significant changes to his lifestyle. These choices and behaviors resulted in his recovery to full health and many more vibrant years.

My father's life embodies both good and bad fortune as well as good and bad luck, a reminder that they are so often intertwined. A cruel turn of events, whether it is a global crisis or a personal health emergency, is terribly unfortunate. It also pushes you out of your comfort zone and forces you to make choices, some of which unlock extraordinary luck. My father still believes that he is incredibly lucky, and I remind him that his luck has been the result of many factors, many of which were under his control.

I hope this book has convinced you that even amid great difficulty, there are often ways to harness the winds of luck, however faint or fleeting they may be. You can't control when and where those winds blow, or how strong they are, but you can construct your ship, recruit your crew, and hoist your sail to search for lucky breaks. Luck isn't something that just happens to you. It results from your preparation, the team you've built, and a set of skills that can be learned and mastered with practice.

Once you start looking, you will see examples every-where—in movies, articles, and everyday actions of those you know. One of my favorite fictional examples of catching the winds of luck comes from Dorothy in *The Wizard of Oz.*[6] Her story begins with pure misfortune. A tornado rips through her world, hurls her house high in the air, and throws her into the unknown. Thrust into the disorienting world of Oz, complete with fanciful characters and a wicked witch, Dorothy strives to find her way back home to Kansas by harnessing luck along the way.

Along her journey on the Yellow Brick Road to Oz in search of the all-powerful wizard, Dorothy learns to cultivate courage, ask for what she needs, help others along the way, build trust, take bold risks, and stay true to her purpose—her personal North Star. Each step, each relationship, and each act of bravery allows her to capture a little more luck. In the end, it isn't magic that brings Dorothy back to Kansas but rather the accumulation of the choices she made, the people she supported, and the strength she discovered in herself that allowed her to catch the winds of luck that literally carried her home.

Remember, there is a world of difference between fortune—the things that happen to you—and luck—the opportunities that you create. We are always engaged in a dance with the world, trading off who is leading and who is following. Sometimes fortune delivers us favors. Sometimes it serves us setbacks. Even then, you retain the power to respond by adjusting your course, patching your sails, and staying in motion.

Luck is a long game that compounds over time. So, construct your ship by preparing your mind, recruit your crew by developing trusting relationships, and hoist your sail by doing the hard work of seizing opportunities as they blow by. Luck, like the wind, is always there. It is invisible but ever present, ready to be caught and capable of carrying you far, transforming your aspirations into tangible achievements.

Catch the Winds of Luck

Construct Your Ship

Values—Luck favors those whose values keep them steady in turbulent waters.

Story—Luck favors those whose personal narrative carries them toward favorable seas.

Risk—Luck favors those who know their limits and dare to sail past them.

Skills—Luck favors those who develop abilities that increase the size of their sail.

Goals—Luck favors those with clear goals, pointing them toward their objectives.

Recruit Your Crew

Ask—Luck favors those who know what they want and ask for it clearly.

Appreciate—Luck favors those who give thanks; goodwill grows into good fortune.

Give—Luck favors the generous; goodwill sows the seeds of serendipity.

Trust—Luck favors those who build trust, an invisible force that draws opportunity closer.

Resolve—Luck favors those who untangle the knots that tether opportunities.

Hoist Your Sail

Experiment—Luck favors those who stir the pot, creating room for surprises.

Jump—Luck favors those who take risks, each one a stepping stone toward success.

Leverage—Luck favors those who build on tiny victories, creating ladders to larger wins.

Question—Luck favors those who ask questions, each one baiting good fortune to bite.

Bounce—Luck favors the resilient, who turn setbacks into second chances.

Innovate—Luck favors those who see problems as opportunities for creative solutions.

Prioritize—Luck favors those who say no, clearing clutter from the road to success.

Stretch—Luck favors those who embrace imposter syndrome as fortune forms at the frontier.

ACKNOWLEDGMENTS

I am incredibly lucky to have such a wonderful crew involved in bringing this book to life!

Big thanks go to all those who shared their stories with me, including current students, alumni, friends, family, and colleagues: Matt Abrahams, Monique Anton, Peter Anton, Azza Cohen, Andrew Couch, Mariano-Florentino Cuéllar, Rawan Dareer, Batu Demir, David Eagleman, Katherine Emery, Drew Endy, Sarahi Espinoza Salamanca, Nir Eyal, Sonia Garcia, Thay Graciano, Oliver Greenwald, Rachel Greenwald, Martin Hellman, Grace Isford, Bhav Jain, Mykel Kochenderfer, Aya Mouallem, Beverly Parenti, Danit Peleg, Somik Raha, Chris Redlitz, Heidi Roizen, Robert Sapolsky, Alberto Savoia, Lisa Kay Solomon, Sarah Soule, Piya Sorcar, Michael Tennefoss, Tenaya West, Janine Zacharia, Barkotel Zemenu, and Anson Zhou.

Once the first draft was complete, I drew upon the guidance from several people who read the manuscript carefully and gave me helpful feedback on the framework, the structure of the book, and the prose. This includes Thay Graciano, Oliver Greenwald, John Hennessy, Stacy

Peña, Josh Tennefoss, Michael Tennefoss, Eric Volmar, and Barkotel Zemenu.

A huge shoutout goes to my husband, Michael, who is always my final reviewer before I submit a manuscript. He treats each and every sentence with the same amount of care as he combs through the text. After eighteen books, I have finally grown to love the wealth of feedback that he provides. ☺ Besides his editorial prowess, Mike is the best life partner one could ever imagine. This book will come out on the eve of our fortieth anniversary. Happy anniversary, Mike!

Thanks go to my colleagues and students at Stanford's Knight-Hennessy Scholars. I am so lucky to get to work with all of them! Each day brings new opportunities to learn and grow as a person and a leader in our dynamic community. I am beyond indebted to John Hennessy, who inspires me every day, for inviting me to join the team five years ago. Every day, I wake up excited to work on our important mission to prepare the next generation of global leaders. And, important recognition goes to Tom Byers, who took a risk in hiring me at Stanford twenty-five years ago, and whose mentorship and support have been immeasurable.

Special mention goes to Oliver Greenwald, whose story is shared in chapter 12 on *Inviting Luck*. As written, Oliver reached out to me after watching my TED Talk on luck and wanted my guidance on how to become a luck coach. We set up a time to talk, where I helped him with his idea and he shared personal examples that ended up in this book. BUT, it didn't stop there. Oliver sent me a thoughtful thank-you note as well as a long list of ways he could help me with this book, which I had just started writing. I was so taken with his initiative that I hired Oliver as a research assistant for this book. It was a joy to work with him. Additionally, this story echoes the ideas in the chapters on asking for what you want, helping others, showing appreciation, and building on small wins.

This book would never have come to life without my wonderful colleagues at HarperCollins, including my editor, Nina Shield. Her enthusiasm for this project has been so motivating throughout the process. I deeply appreciate her remarkable responsiveness and attention to every detail. In addition, I truly value the contributions of copyeditor Emily Wichland, who expertly polished the prose and made sure all the references are correct. There are also so many others at HarperCollins whose talent and attention contributed to this book, including Daphney Guillaume, Lisa Zuniga, Marta Durkin, Yvonne Chan, Jason Kayser, Courtney Nobile, Ashley Yepsen, and Stephen Callahan.

Thanks to my father, Jerry Seelig, for serving as the provocateur for this book, starting when I was a little girl. I can't count the number of times he said, "The harder I work, the luckier I get." I am so fortunate to have learned so much from him, and know that this book will open the door to many more conversations, aka debates, about the role of luck in our lives. Here's to Papa on his hundredth birthday!

To all those who are reading this book, thank you for taking the time to explore ways to bring more luck into your life. I hope that some of the ideas resonate with you, and that you feel more empowered to create the future you dream to live.

As a final provocation, I invite you to keep a fortune and luck résumé to chronicle both what arrives unexpectedly and what you consciously cultivate. Hopefully, after reading this book, you will be able to add many more items to your luck list as your life unfolds!

NOTES

Introduction: Catching the Winds of Luck

1. *Oxford English Dictionary*, "luck," accessed June 27, 2025, https://www.oed.com/dictionary/luck_n.
2. Wikipedia, "Serendipity," last modified June 13, 2025, https://en.wikipedia.org/wiki/Serendipity.
3. Elizabeth Jamison Hodges, *The Three Princes of Serendip* (Atheneum, 1964).
4. Post-it® Brand, "Contact Us," Post-it (website), accessed June 27, 2025, https://www.post-it.com/3M/en_US/post-it/contact-us/about-us/.
5. "The Legend of Picasso's Napkin Sketch," *Paintvine* (blog), accessed June 27, 2025, https://paintvine.co.nz/blogs/news/the-legend-of-picassos-napkin-sketch.
6. Renamed the San Quentin Rehabilitation Center in 2023.
7. Michael W. Kraus, Stéphane Côté, and Dacher Keltner, "Social Class, Contextualism, and Empathic Accuracy," *Psychological Science* 21, no. 11 (November 2010): 1716–23, https://doi.org/10.1177/0956797610387613.
8. Viktor E. Frankl, *Man's Search for Meaning* (Beacon Press, 2006).
9. Editors of Encyclopaedia Britannica, "Fortuna," *Britannica*, accessed June 27, 2025, https://www.britannica.com/topic/Fortuna-Roman-goddess.

10. Grace Mannon, "9 Traditional New Year's Foods to Eat for Good Luck," *Taste of Home*, last updated September 24, 2024, https://www.tasteofhome.com/collection/new-years-day-food-good-luck/.

11. NASA Science Editorial Team, "What Are JPL's Lucky Peanuts?," *NASA Science*, October 15, 2021, https://science.nasa.gov/missions/what-are-jpls-lucky-peanuts/.

12. Robert Sapolsky, *Determined* (Penguin Press, 2023).

13. Peter R. Darke and Jonathan L. Freedman, "The Belief in Good Luck Scale," *Journal of Research in Personality* 31, no. 4 (December 1997): 486–511.

14. Richard Wiseman, *The Luck Factor: Changing Your Luck, Changing Your Life–The Four Essential Principles* (Miramax/Hyperion, 2003).

15. In some cases, I am only using their first names, based on each person's wishes.

Chapter 1: Build Your Ballast

1. Daniel Kahneman, *Thinking, Fast and Slow* (Farrar, Straus and Giroux, 2011).

2. Jonathan Haidt, *The Happiness Hypothesis: Finding Modern Truth in Ancient Wisdom* (Basic Books, 2006).

3. Robert B. Cialdini, *Influence: The Psychology of Persuasion*, rev. ed. (Harper Business, 2007).

4. James M. Kouzes and Barry Z. Posner, *The Five Practices of Exemplary Leadership*, 2nd ed. (John Wiley & Sons, 2011).

5. Bill George and Natalie Kindred, "Daniel Kim's Dilemma (A)," Harvard Business School Case 411–009, Harvard Business School Case Collection, April 2011.

6. Somik Raha, *Invaluable: Achieving Clarity on Value* (Invaluable Books, 2023).

7. "Elizabeth Holmes," Profile, *Forbes*, accessed November 20, 2025, https://www.forbes.com/profile/elizabeth-holmes/.

Chapter 2: Tell Your Tale

1. Stanford d.school is a nickname for the Hasso Plattner Institute of Design at Stanford: dschool.stanford.edu.
2. Brian Lowery, *Selfless: The Social Creation of "You"* (Harper, 2023).
3. Brian Lowery, "You May Not Be Who You Think You Are," *Stanford Graduate School of Business Insights*, https://www.gsb.stanford.edu/insights/you-may-not-be-who-you-think-you-are.
4. Dan P. McAdams, "Personal Narratives and the Life Story," in *Handbook of Personality: Theory and Research*, 3rd ed., eds. Oliver P. John, Richard W. Robins, and Lawrence A. Pervin (Guilford Press, 2008), 242–62.
5. Timothy D. Wilson, *Redirect: The Surprising New Science of Psychological Change* (Little, Brown, 2011).
6. Carol S. Dweck, *Mindset: The New Psychology of Success* (Random House, 2006).

Chapter 3: Cultivate Courage

1. Tina Seelig, *What I Wish I Knew When I Was 20: A Crash Course on Making Your Place in the World*, 10th anniversary ed. (HarperOne, 2019).
2. Jim Collins and Morten T. Hansen, *Great by Choice: Uncertainty, Chaos, and Luck—Why Some Thrive Despite Them All* (Harper Business, 2011).
3. Jeff Bezos, "2016 Letter to Shareholders," About Amazon, April 17, 2017, https://www.aboutamazon.com/news/company-news/2016-letter-to-shareholders.

Notes

Chapter 4: Expand Your Sail

1. Malcolm Gladwell, *Outliers: The Story of Success* (Little, Brown, 2008).
2. Anders Ericsson and Robert Pool, *Peak: Secrets from the New Science of Expertise* (Houghton Mifflin Harcourt, 2016).
3. Tom Rath, *StrengthsFinder 2.0* (Gallup Press, 2007).

Chapter 5: Set Your North Star

1. "Our Story," Amae Health, https://www.amaehealth.com/.
2. Edwin A. Locke and Gary P. Latham, "Building a Practically Useful Theory of Goal Setting and Task Motivation: A 35-Year Odyssey," *American Psychologist* 57, no. 9 (2002): 705–17.

Chapter 6: Ask for Luck

1. Adam Grant, *Give and Take: A Revolutionary Approach to Success* (Viking, 2013).

Chapter 7: Appreciate Luck

1. Robert A. Emmons, *Gratitude Works!: A 21-Day Program for Creating Emotional Prosperity* (Jossey-Bass, 2013).
2. Melissa Madeson, "The Neuroscience of Gratitude and Its Effects on the Brain," PositivePsychology.com, September 15, 2025, https://positivepsychology.com/neuroscience-of-gratitude/.
3. Geyze Diniz, Ligia Korkes, Luca Schiliró Tristão, Rosangela Pelegrini, Patrícia Lacerda Bellodi, and Wanderly Marques Bernardo, "The Effects of Gratitude Interventions: A Systematic Review and Meta-Analysis," *Einstein (São Paulo)* 21 (2023): eRW0371, https://doi.org/10.31744/einstein_journal/2023RW0371.

4. Joshua W. Brown and Y. Joel Wong, "How Gratitude Changes You and Your Brain," *Greater Good Magazine*, June 6, 2017, https://greatergood.berkeley.edu/article/item/how _gratitude_changes_you_and_your_brain. greatergood .berkeley.edu+3.

5. Polly Campbell, "Gratitude Could Help Your Marriage Last," *Psychology Today*, October 27, 2023, https://www.psychology today.com/us/blog/imperfect-spirituality/202310/gratitude -could-help-your-marriage-last.

6. Jill Suttie, "The Ripple Effects of a Thank You," *Greater Good Magazine*, December 20, 2019, https://greatergood.berkeley.edu /article/item/the_ripple_effects_of_a_thank_you.

7. Jay Reeves, "How Thank-You Notes Saved a Dying Company," *Lawyers Mutual*, January 25, 2016, https://lawyersmutualnc.com /article/how-thank-you-notes-saved-a-dying-company/.

8. "The Campbell Soup Story," ConantLeadership, October 4, 2023, https://conantleadership.com/the-campbell-soup-story/#close.

9. Robin Dunbar, *Grooming, Gossip, and the Evolution of Language* (Harvard University Press, 1996).

Chapter 8: Give Away Luck

1. Nir and Far, https://app.usemotion.com/meet/nir-eyal /4dl1y?d=30.

2. Knight-Hennessy Scholars, *Lessons in Leadership*, August 14, 2024, https://knight-hennessy.stanford.edu/news/lessons -leadership.

3. Robert B. Cialdini, *Influence: The Psychology of Persuasion*, rev. ed. (Harper Business, 2007).

4. Monica Y. Bartlett and David DeSteno, "Gratitude and Prosocial Behavior: Helping When It Costs You," *Psychological Science* 17, no. 4 (May 2006): 319–25.

5. Adam Grant, *Give and Take: Why Helping Others Drives Our Success* (Viking, 2013).
6. All Girls Code, https://www.allgirlscode.me/.

Chapter 9: Attract Luck

1. Mark S. Granovetter, "The Strength of Weak Ties," *American Journal of Sociology* 78, no. 6 (May 1973): 1360–80.
2. Stephen M. R. Covey, *The Speed of Trust: The One Thing That Changes Everything* (Free Press, 2006).
3. Adam Bryant, "Questback's Lead Strategist on His 'User Manual,'" *The New York Times*, March 30, 2013, https://www.nytimes.com/2013/03/31/business/questbacks-lead-strategist-on-his-user-manual.html.
4. Daniel Jones, "The 36 Questions That Lead to Love," *The New York Times*, January 9, 2015.
5. Jamil Zaki, *Hope for Cynics: The Surprising Science of Human Goodness* (Grand Central Publishing, 2024).

Chapter 10: Unshackle Luck

1. Bart Verkuil, Jos F. Brosschot, W. A. Gebhardt, and Julian F. Thayer, "When Worries Make You Sick: A Review of Perseverative Cognition, the Default Stress Response and Somatic Health," *Journal of Experimental Psychopathology* 1, no. 1 (2010), https://doi.org/10.5127/jep.009110.
2. Robert M. Sapolsky, *Why Zebras Don't Get Ulcers: The Acclaimed Guide to Stress, Stress-Related Diseases, and Coping* (Henry Holt, 2004).
3. Dorothie L. Hellman and Martin E. Hellman, *A New Map for Relationships: Creating True Love at Home and Peace on the Planet* (New Map Publishing, 2016).

4. Hellman, *A New Map for Relationships*, 3–5.
5. Alain de Botton, *The Course of Love: A Novel* (Signal Books, 2016).
6. Fred Luskin, *Forgive for Good: A Proven Prescription for Health and Happiness*, reprint ed. (HarperOne, 2003).

Chapter 12: Invite Luck

1. Matt Haig, *The Midnight Library: A Novel* (Viking, 2020).
2. Stuart Kauffman, *Investigations* (Oxford University Press, 2000).

Chapter 14: Capture Luck

1. Burkhard Bilger, "The Possibilian," *The New Yorker*, April 18, 2011, https://www.newyorker.com/magazine/2011/04/25/the-possibilian.
2. David Eagleman, *Sum: Forty Tales from the Afterlives* (Pantheon Books, 2009).
3. David Epstein, *Range: Why Generalists Triumph in a Specialized World* (Riverhead Books, 2019).
4. Debra Schifrin, "4 Listening Skills Leaders Need to Master," *Harvard Business Review*, December 16, 2024, https://hbr.org/2024/12/4-listening-skills-leaders-need-to-master.
5. Olivia Fox Cabane, *The Charisma Myth: How Anyone Can Master the Art and Science of Personal Magnetism* (Portfolio, 2012).

Chapter 15: Rebound to Luck

1. Karen Reivich and Andrew Shatté, *The Resilience Factor: 7 Essential Skills for Overcoming Life's Inevitable Obstacles* (Broadway Books, 2002).

Chapter 16: Invent Luck

1. Tina Seelig, "A Month of Tiny Teaching 'Jolts,'" *Medium* (Stanford d.school), May 31, 2020, https://medium.com/stanford-d-school/a-month-of-tiny-teaching-jolts-a2bdf8ab97d7.
2. Sarah Waldorf and Annelisa Stephan, "Getty Artworks Re-created with Household Items by Creative Geniuses the World Over," Getty, March 30, 2020, https://www.getty.edu/news/getty-artworks-recreated-with-household-items-by-creative-geniuses-the-world-over/.
3. Danit Peleg, Danit Peleg–3D Printed Fashion Lab (website), https://www.danitpeleg.com/.

Chapter 17: Prioritize Luck

1. Will Durant, *The Story of Philosophy: The Lives and Opinions of the World's Greatest Philosophers* (Simon & Schuster, 1926).
2. Greg McKeown, *Essentialism: The Disciplined Pursuit of Less* (Crown Business, 2014).
3. Julian Givi and Colleen P. Kirk, "Saying No: The Negative Ramifications from Invitation Declines Are Less Severe Than We Think," *Journal of Personality and Social Psychology* 126, no. 6 (2024): 1103–15, https://doi.org/10.1037/pspi0000443.
4. American Psychological Association, "Just Say No to That Invitation: It May Feel Unforgivably Rude to Reject an Invitation—Even One to an Event You Would Much Prefer Not to Attend," *American Psychological Association News*, December 2023, https://www.apa.org/news/press/releases/2023/12/say-no-invitation.

Chapter 18: Stretch Toward Luck

1. Matt Abrahams, *Speaking Up without Freaking Out: 50 Techniques for Confident and Compelling Presenting*, 3rd ed. (Kendall Hunt Publishing, 2016).

2. Suzy Kassem, *Rise Up and Salute the Sun: The Writings of Suzy Kassem* (CreateSpace Independent Publishing, 2010).
3. Dena M. Bravata et al., "Prevalence, Predictors, and Treatment of Impostor Syndrome: A Systematic Review," *Journal of General Internal Medicine* 35, no. 4 (2020): 1252–75.

Conclusion: Luck Is a Long Game

1. Robert B. Cialdini, *Influence, New and Expanded: The Psychology of Persuasion* (Harper Business, 2021).
2. Martin E. P. Seligman, *Helplessness: On Depression, Development, and Death* (W. H. Freeman, 1975).
3. Lyn Y. Abramson, Martin E. P. Seligman, and John D. Teasdale, "Learned Helplessness in Humans: Critique and Reformulation," *Journal of Abnormal Psychology* 87, no. 1 (1978): 49–74.
4. Martin E. P. Seligman, *Learned Optimism: How to Change Your Mind and Your Life* (Free Press, 1990).
5. Seligman, *Helplessness*.
6. *The Wizard of Oz*, directed by Victor Fleming, featuring Judy Garland, Frank Morgan, Ray Bolger, Bert Lahr, and Jack Haley (Metro-Goldwyn-Mayer, 1939).

INDEX

Index

Index

Index

Index

Index

Index

Index

Index

Index

ABOUT THE AUTHOR

Tina Seelig has taught at Stanford University for more than twenty-five years. She is executive director of Knight-Hennessy Scholars, a leadership program for graduate students across the university, and faculty director emerita of the Stanford Technology Ventures Program, the entrepreneurship center at Stanford School of Engineering. She has taught many courses on creative problem solving in the Hasso Plattner Institute of Design (Stanford d.school) for over two decades.

Dr. Seelig earned her PhD in neuroscience at Stanford Medical School, and has been a management consultant, entrepreneur, and author of eighteen books and games, including *inGenius*, *Creativity Rules*, and *What I Wish I Knew When I Was 20*.

She is the recipient of the Gordon Prize from the National Academy of Engineering, recognizing her as a national leader in engineering education; the Olympus Innovation Award; the Silicon Valley Visionary Award; and the Global Consortium of Entrepreneurship Centers Legacy Award.

MORE
INSIGHT AND WISDOM
FROM
TINA SEELIG

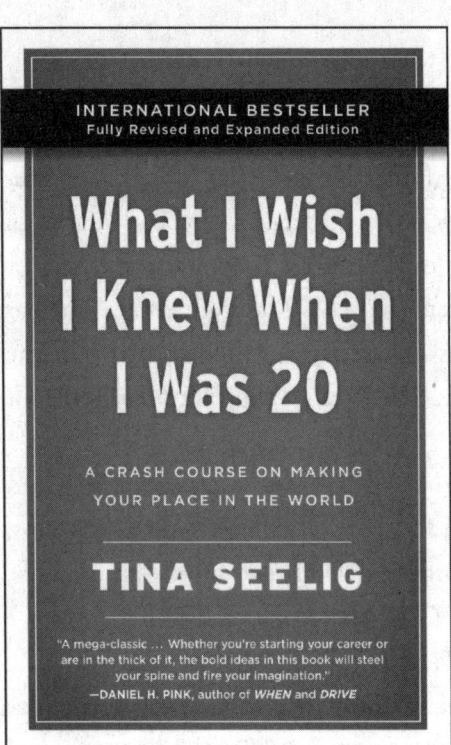

AVAILABLE WHEREVER BOOKS, EBOOKS, AND AUDIOBOOKS ARE SOLD